The London Garden Book A-Z

Abigail Willis

The London Garden Book A-Z

Written by Abigail Willis
Photography by Andrew Kershman, Susi Koch, Abigail Willis and Stephen Millar
Edited by Andrew Kershman
Book design by Lesley Gilmour & Susi Koch
Illustrations and cover design by Lesley Gilmour

Published in 2012 by
Metro Publications Ltd, PO Box 6336, London, N1 6PY

Metro® is a registered trade mark of Associated Newspapers Limited.
The METRO mark is under licence from Associated Newspapers Limited.

Printed and bound in India.
This book is produced using paper from registered sustainable
and managed sources. Suppliers have provided both LEI and
MUTU certification.

ISBN 978-1-902910-42-0

LONDON GARDEN HISTORY

London Garden History

With over 3,000 parks and open spaces covering some 67 square miles, London is revered as one of the world's greenest capitals. But famous as they are, London's parks are only one aspect of the city's green and pleasant demeanour – Greater London contains an estimated 3.8 million domestic gardens, covering one fifth of its area. It is also home to an impressive array of publicly accessible gardens, such as the centuries-old, former monastic gardens belonging to Westminster College (see p.230) and Inner Temple (see p.134). Even London's squares and cemeteries often have the prefix 'garden' attached to them, suggesting the capital's fondness for informal, domestic style open spaces.

At the heart of royal and fashionable court life, and the trade hub of an expanding Empire, London was naturally a centre for high-powered gardening. The

Westminster College Garden

hottest design trends and the latest plant discoveries landed in London first, and it was in London's botanic gardens, nurseries and private homes that new species were raised, studied and tended, endowing English gardeners with a degree of plantsmanship that was admired throughout Europe.

From the late 16th century the capital's busy river wharves and docks received an influx of exciting plant discoveries from the Levant and the Americas. The John Tradescants, a father and son gardening duo who successively held the post of *Keeper of his Majesty's Gardens, Vines and Silkworms*, were each responsible for several new introductions and their well-stocked garden in Lambeth became a London landmark. *Tradescantia virginiana* is named in honour of Tradescant the Elder, while it is the Younger that we must thank for Michaelmas daisies, phlox and magnolia.

Taking up the Tradescants' mantle, 18th-century London merchant Peter Collinson was the conduit for many American plant species entering British gardens, working in collaboration with the Philadelphia-based botanist John Bartram. Collinson employed Bartram to seek out new species, the seeds of which were duly shipped over to London and distributed to subscribers. Loddiges' Nursery in Hackney and Philip Miller, head gardener at the Chelsea Physic Garden, were among the pioneers who subscribed to 'Bartram's boxes', the first of which arrived in London in 1734. At Osterley Park a special 'American border' was created to showcase newly discovered North American trees, shrubs and flowers, ordered by Osterley's plant-collecting châtelaine, Mrs Child.

This being the Age of Reason, serious research accompanied the quest for novelty and London became home to a succession of horticultural establishments such as the Chelsea Physic Garden (founded 1673, see p.56) and the Royal Botanic Gardens at Kew (established 1757, see p.208). The

Chelsea Physic Garden

Horticultural Society of London was set up in 1804 with the aim of collecting plant information and encouraging best horticultural practice, and became the Royal Horticultural Society in 1861. Among its eminent founder members were the botanist Sir Joseph Banks and royal head gardener William Forsyth – the Society's first meeting was held at Hatchard's Bookshop, on Piccadilly.

It was in London too that modern horticultural literature was born, with early publications including the list published in 1596 by John Gerard of the plants in his Holborn garden and *Paradisi in Sole Paradisus Terrestris,* a horticultural manual written in 1629 by the apothecary John Parkinson, who had a sizeable botanic garden in Long Acre. Although the Deptford based diarist John Evelyn failed to complete his great work on British gardening, the *Elysium Britannicum,* his published works include the *Kalendarium Hortense* of 1664 (one of the earliest gardening almanacs) and a monograph on salads. The book was published in 1699 and includes Evelyn's recipe for salad dressing – revealing that the culinary use of olive oil in British households was by no means a 1960's innovation.

The emergence of the terraced house with its enclosed back (and sometimes front) garden as London's default residential unit during the city's rapid expansion in the 18th and 19th centuries really turned London into a city of gardeners. With their own little patch of London soil to cultivate,

Thomas Carlyle's Garden, see p.46

The Hill Garden & Pergola, see p.128

Londoners got busy planning and planting beds, enthused by practical guides such as Thomas Fairchild's 1722 publication *The City Gardener,* written specifically for a London audience. London's infamous smog made growing conditions difficult for most plants (they usually died after flowering), but this obsolescence suited the city's burgeoning nursery trade and those such as Loddiges' and James Gordon's in Mile End did a roaring trade. Carlyle's House in Chelsea (see p.46) displays a typical London back garden layout of the 19th century (although the house itself dates from the previous century).

The rustic and romantic Arts and Crafts garden developed by William Robinson and Gertrude Jekyll was the dominant garden style of the late 19th and early 20th centuries. Essentially designed for a country house setting, the style could be transplanted to the city but only by those wealthy enough to afford the generous plots of land it demanded. In London, two delightful essays in the style are The Hill Garden and Pergola (see p.129), designed by TH Mawson for Lord Leverhulme, and Eltham Palace (see p.90), whose Arts & Crafts gardens temper the Art Deco glamour of the Palace's interiors, installed by the millionaire couple Stephen and Virginia Courtauld. The masses were also able to enjoy a taste of this gracious style of gardening thanks to JJ Sexby, who was appointed London County Council's first superintendant of Parks in 1889. Sexby installed 'Old English Gardens' in several of the parks he laid out, including

The Walled Garden, Brockwell Park - see p.228

Peckham Rye Park, Southwark Park and Brockwell Park – whose Sexby-designed walled garden has recently been restored (see p.228).

Gardening became a national necessity during the two world wars of the 20th century, when food shortages prompted a huge increase in allotment plots and motivated the population to 'dig for victory'. In London the Blitz was a catalyst for early community gardens, with some bomb sites being turned into impromptu gardens by local workers and residents. A few became permanent fixtures and former bomb sites in the City, such as the Goldsmiths' Garden (see p.148) and the Cleary Garden (see p.69), flourish to this day (although considerably smartened up since their original make-do-and-mend guise). The desire to cultivate derelict land lives on in 21st century London, in community enterprises such as Bonnington Square (see p.28) and Culpeper Community Garden (see p.86), or in guerrilla gardens like the Lavender Field in Lambeth (see p.112).

The current surge in popularity of gardening as a pastime has been accompanied by a growing appreciation of London's horticultural heritage. Two of London's most significant gardens have recently been the subject of extensive restorations – Chiswick House (see p.60), the birthplace of the Landscape Movement, and Myddelton House Garden (see p.160), the home of renowned 20th-century plantsman, E A Bowles. It is surely no coincidence that the first museum in the world to be devoted to garden history should be in London, and more precisely in Lambeth, one-time home to the pioneering, plant-hunting Tradescants. A celebration of four centuries of British gardening, the Garden Museum (see p.102) is a fine place to start any exploration of London's gardens.

Thames Barrier Park, see p.210

LONDON GARDENS A-Z

Golf Course Allotments, Haringey

A Allotments

After years in the doldrums allotment gardening is back on the agenda – and in a big way. In London demand far outstrips supply, with some boroughs' waiting lists stretching far into the future (Wandsworth has one of the longest in the country) while others, such as Hackney, have closed their lists altogether.

History has shown that when the going gets tough, the tough get digging, and UK allotment numbers peaked at 1.75 million during the 'dig for victory years' of WWII. Today, runaway food prices, concerns about food security, pesticides and the dominance of supermarkets, have all contributed to the resurgence of allotment gardening. The quaint, old-fashioned concept of eating fresh food in season has also made a comeback, along with a desire to cut food miles, 'eat local' and reconnect with nature.

Those lucky enough to have an allotment can't rest on their laurels though, since according to a government report (commissioned in 2006, but buried until 2011) the number of UK allotments fell by over 50,000 in the previous decade; they currently stand at around 250,000. On this land-limited island of ours even allotments with 'statutory' (as opposed to 'temporary') status aren't guaranteed protection. In London, where pressure on open space is acute, allotments have been at the centre of some notable planning battles. Manor Gardens allotments in east London, which had been bequeathed in perpetuity for the benefit of local people in 1900 by Major Arthur Villiers, were obliterated in 2007 to make way for the new Olympic Park, despite a strong campaign to save them. But bulldozers aren't always a foregone conclusion and in 2010, allotmenteers at Fortis Green were able to buy their site from their landlord, Thames Water, thus saving it from development. The site is now run by the Fortis Green Community Allotments Trust.

Much cherished by their members, London's allotments are vibrant, multicultural, cross-generational mini-communities. Some sites are more utilitarian than others, but some lucky plot-holders can enjoy mod-cons such as composting toilets, cafés, trading huts, manure bins, wildlife areas and events such as seed swaps, barbecues, flower shows, and even horticultural speed-dating. Most allotments are usually closed to the public but some – such as the Golf Course Allotments in Haringey – participate in the NGS Open Gardens scheme (see The Yellow Book, p.264) and the London Open Garden Square Weekend in June (see p.170) allowing visitors to see behind the scenes of these productive urban plots. It's always fascinating to observe so many different approaches to growing in one place – even if everyone else's veg invariably looks healthier than your own.

At Stanley Road Allotments in Sutton, visitors can even take part in the harvest, since the site shares 3 of its 10 acres with Carshalton Lavender, a not for profit community project devoted to reviving the once thriving, centuries old, local lavender industry. The volunteer-run project, which was set up in 1996, celebrated its first harvest in 2001 and in 2009 distilled the first lavender oil in Carshalton for a century. Impressively, the field was entirely stocked with plants grown from locally sourced cuttings of *Lavandula intermedia*, believed to be from the original lavender fields. The project continues to offer plenty of scope for involvement, from regular workdays and foster-a-cutting schemes, to the Community Harvest at the end of the July, when the field is opened to the public to pick their own lavender.

And this being London, even humble allotment sites with their patchwork of plots and ramshackle sheds can come dripping in history, such as those at Fulham Palace Meadows, founded in 1916 on a site that previously played host to Roman, Anglo-Saxon and Viking settlements. The Royal Paddocks allotments at Bushy Park have an even grander provenance, having been granted to the 'labouring poor' by Royal Warrant in 1921 on Crown land formerly used as paddocks for the king's horses. In Brixton the 26 plots of the Windmill Allotments flourish in the shadow of a recently restored historic 19th-century windmill; while in Hampstead, the Branch Hill allotments are picturesquely sited on the former garden of the mansion belonging to John Spedon Lewis, founder of John Lewis stores – the 32 plots here are presumably 'never knowingly under-sowed'.

Getting an Allotment

Those in search of a plot of their own should contact their local borough council in the first instance, since most allotments are council owned and restricted to local residents. The London Allotments Network is a useful second port of call and holds a waiting list of people who want plots and who live in boroughs where there are no allotments or who are already on a borough waiting list but prepared to take a plot in another borough.

However, there's no need to sit idly by while you grow old waiting for an allotment to become vacant. A number of local and national initiatives (such as the Landshare social network) aim to get people growing food without the need for an allotment. Working with the charity Age UK, Wandsworth Council has set up Garden Partners, a scheme that teams up garden owners over the age of 60 with volunteers who wish to tend a garden regularly, with the 'partners' sharing any fruit or vegetables grown. The Wimbledon Food Group also runs a garden share scheme and has developed two community gardens in the borough, The Christchurch Garden and the Fireplace Community Garden. Other schemes designed to circumnavigate the shortage of food-growing land in London are Food up Front and Capital Growth (see p.38), the latter being a dynamic and ambitious scheme run by London Food Link to create 2012 new growing spaces in London by the end of 2012.

King Henry's Walk Garden

Resources in brief

Cable Street Community Garden

"*Regular deliveries of horse manure from the police stables nearby keeps the soil fertility levels high.*"

Cable Street Community Gardens

With its patchwork of productive plots enclosed by residential buildings and the brick arches of a railway bridge, the Cable Street Community Garden is a latter day, inner city version of the traditional walled kitchen garden. These gardens however were never an adjunct to a big house, but were created in the 1970s as a far-sighted Friends of the Earth initiative to reclaim derelict land for community use. From the early days of a few dedicated pioneers, the gardens have grown in popularity and today boast around 100 members, of all ages, different walks of life and cultural backgrounds.

The gardens have always been run organically and over the decades have developed a lively biodiversity, nurtured by the absence of pesticides, the wide range of vegetables, fruit and flowers grown on site, and by wildlife friendly features such as ponds, wildflowers areas and a native hedgerow. Two bee hives have recently been introduced, and are looked after by long-standing member Jane O'Sullivan and Emir Hasham, a plotholder for 4 years. One hive is tucked away on Emir's spacious plot by the railways arches with the bees being housed in a plastic modern hive, the 'Beehaus' made by Omlet. As a new beekeeper he finds this design easy to use and the bees settled in well. The allotment is Emir's relaxation away from his career working in special effects for TV advertising – 'I try to grow things that I like eating but that look nice as well.' His eclectic choice of crops includes chillies, peppers and aubergines, black kale, several varieties of chicory, a kiwi fruit and hops.

www.cablestreetcommunitygardens.co.uk
www.omlet.co.uk

Emir Hasham

As divisive as Marmite, this residential quarter in the heart of the City, has attracted more than its fair share of criticism since its official opening in 1982. It is now recognised as a bona fide architectural icon, having been listed (Grade II*) by English Heritage in 2001.

It's all too easy to dismiss the Barbican as a concrete carbuncle but the Brutalist vision of architects Chamberlain, Powell and Bon is actually a good deal greener than is often credited. Over half the Estate's 15.2 hectares is open space, of which 5.25 hectares is given over to public and private landscaped gardens, lakes and the Conservatory. There are potentially 12 kilometres of window boxes and residents deploy these to great effect, while the highwalks are punctuated with wooden tubs and concrete troughs gardened by the City of London and members of the Barbican Horticultural Society respectively. Some containers serve as resident's allotments and their rows of Swiss chard, onions, asparagus and beetroot strike a homely note on the ultra urban highwalks.

Although Le Corbusier's Unité d'Habitation was a strong influence on Chamberlain, Powell and Bon's Barbican designs, the classic London garden square was also a reference point.

"The Barbican Conservatory is less well known, despite being the second largest of its kind in London after Kew."

" *There are potentially 12km of window boxes...* "

Thomas More Garden and Speed Gardens (the Barbican's two private gardens), are defined by the surrounding residential blocks. Beech Garden, a publicly accessible garden, follows a similar format but is effectively a container garden on a large scale, made up of formal beds let into the tiled surface of the Barbican's 'podium' level. The garden's luxuriant specimen trees such as *Morus nigra* and *Liquidamber*, make it hard to believe that the maximum planting depth here is only 3 feet.

Probably the best-known public open space in the Barbican is the Lakeside Terrace in front of the Arts Centre. Here visitors experience the Barbican's hard landscaping at its most uncompromising, although softened slightly by containerised palm trees and the shallow green waters of the lake. The latter is planted with yellow flag iris and is home to shoals of rudd and golden orfe (the carp who previously lived in the lake fell victim to a pike).

The Barbican Conservatory is less well known, despite being the second largest of its kind in London after Kew. An idiosyncratic afterthought, it was built around the fly tower of the Arts Centre theatre and opened in 1984, with a cacti-filled Arid House being added two years later. The Conservatory is currently open to the public every Sunday 12noon-17.30, offering a chance to admire over 2,000 species of tropical and sub-tropical plants, plus resident terrapins and an aviary.

The Barbican's Fann Street Wildlife Garden is home to wildflowers, small mammals and various bird species and has been designated a site of Borough Importance for Nature Conservation and is managed by the volunteers of the Barbican Wildlife Group. Only open to Barbican residents, the garden usually takes part in the London Open Garden Squares weekend (see p.170). Invertebrates however are free to check in and out of the recently installed insect hotel.

Barbican, Silk St, London, EC2Y 8DS
www.barbican.org.uk   T: 020 7638 4141

Opposite page: Lakeside Terrace / This page: Speed Gardens (above), Lakeside Terrace (below)

Downings Roads Moorings

B Barge Gardens

Garden designers often talk about getting 'movement' into their creations, but on the floating gardens at Downings Roads Moorings the movement is for real, generated by the twice-daily ebb and flow of the Thames and the swell of passing river traffic. For those used to terrestrial gardens the gentle sway can be disconcerting and visitors are advised to wear suitable footwear, and to exercise care when aboard.

The oldest surviving commercial river moorings in London (dating from at least the first half of the 19th century), the Downings Roads Moorings are home today to some 30 river vessels converted to residential or mixed use. Some berth holders tend small gardens on their own boats but the barge gardens themselves are the main attraction, and are constructed on seven Thames lighters (flat-bottomed vessels used for unloading larger vessels). Connected by ingeniously designed bridges, the

garden barges are not just a decorative after-thought: they act as walkways to the individual houseboats as well as accommodating studio apartments.

Architect Nick Lacey is the man behind the Moorings' evolution into a floating garden square (and indeed the gardens do take part in the Open Garden Squares Weekend as well as opening for the NGS). The owner of the moorings, Nick was inspired back in the 80s by seeing a profusion of self-seeded plants growing in a silt-filled lighter and the idea of the barge garden was born. Construction is simple: the lighters are decked over with a steel deck which produces a planting 'tray' about a spit (roughly 25cms) deep; the studio quarters are housed on the lower deck.

Off-shore gardening presents unique challenges and simply getting the soil (a rich 50/50 mix of top-soil and farmyard manure) onto the barges was a major

operation involving a crane and a lot of spadework. Although the river enjoys a mild microclimate, its desiccating winds make watering a constant concern; drought-friendly plants are helpful but nonetheless in dry weather the gardens need watering every other day. During hosepipe bans the gardens are sustained with water pumped from the river which, being silty and full of nutrients, the plants relish.

The barges are planted for year-round interest, with an eclectic mix of trees and shrubs, softened by informal groupings of perennials and self-seeded annuals such as poppies. Trees such as the golden leaved *Robinia frisia* do surprisingly well here, obligingly miniaturising themselves to adapt to the shallow planting depth, and fruit trees such as medlar, apple and plum also thrive. Soil fertility is kept high by regular compost mulches and the odd seaweed dressing.

Attracting a bohemian community of human residents, the barges also appeal to London's wildlife, with ducks, coots, moorhens and geese also making their homes here. Nick is keen to get some bee hives on to the moorings but in the meantime wildlife friendly plants such as nepeta and buddleia keep visiting bees and butterflies in nectar. For their creator, the appeal of the barge gardens lies in their fundamental difference from buildings – for architect Nick, 'what is so wonderful about a garden is that it's organic, it develops, it grows, it changes in a way that buildings find more difficult!'

Downings Roads Moorings
31 Mill Street, SE1 2AX
www.towerbridgemoorings.org
www.ngs.org.uk
www.opensquares.org

ick Lacey

Nick was inspired back in the 80s by seeing a profusion of self-seeded plants growing in a silt-filled lighter and the idea of the barge garden was born.

B Bees

Honey bees may be in decline across the globe but in Britain, at least, the beekeeper population is on the rise – the BBKA's current membership stands at around 22,200, up two-fold since 2005.

In London beekeeping is all the rage, with some 2,500 hives being tended within the M25 and local associations having to temporarily close membership lists as they struggle to cope with the influx of new members. Concern at the plight of *Apis mellifera*, a desire to connect with the rhythms of the natural world and interest in locally produced food are some worthy motivators behind this increase, but it's also true that London is a great place to raise bees. London's status as one of the world's greenest capitals (with over 3,000 parks and open spaces) favours the urban beekeeper, providing a long season of bee-friendly forage, a warm microclimate and a low incidence of the agricultural pesticides used in rural areas.

A symbol of industry and prosperity, it is not surprising that honey bees reside at some of London's most prestigious addresses. The grounds of Buckingham Palace and Clarence House have beehives, as does Regent's Park, while the Fortnum & Mason bees (who live on the roof of the store's Piccadilly premises) live in bespoke, architecturally themed, hives – painted in Fortnum's signature eau de nil. London's cultural institutions have got in on the act too, with the Royal Festival Hall, Tate Modern and Tate Britain and the National Portrait Gallery all keeping bees on their rooftops.

Further east, 8 hives were installed around the Square Mile in 2010 as part of the City Bee Project, with venues including Lloyds of London, St Paul's Cathedral and the Museum of London. To keep its new residents happy, the Museum's courtyard garden (technically a roof garden) has been redesigned and filled with containers of bee-licious plants like heather, buddleia, lavender and verbena while the bee hive itself sits alongside a wildflower 'carpet'. Although these bees are a docile crowd, their hive is set above head height in a fenced off area of the garden, to prevent people disturbing the hive. Looking after the bees is museum visitor host and trainee beekeeper Lynne Connell, assisted by Brian McCallum from Urban Bees, who has been taking Lynne through essential seasonal tasks from winter feeds to checking and treating for the deadly Varroa mite.

Lynne is part of a growing band of fledgling urban beekeepers and she's not alone in having an experienced beekeeper to guide her – the London Beekeepers Association runs its own training programme and recommends that novice beekeepers are mentored for a season before starting a hive of their own. The association's 'training hives' are located at their headquarters at Roots and Shoots (see p.188), where would-be apiarists can learn to handle livestock with a sting in their tale. Regional London beekeeping associations also offer training, as do outfits such as Urban Bees, and the London Honey Company. In Hackney, the Golden Company, whose training hive is based at St Mary's Secret Garden (see p.192), is a social enterprise, training young people in beekeeping and entrepreneurship. Its young 'Bee Guardians' are employed to look after Golden Company hives across the City of London, including high-profile locations such as the London Stock Exchange.

Not everyone can be a beekeeper, but there are other ways in which Londoners can address the potentially disastrous decline in bee numbers. Initiatives such as the Mayor of London's Capital Bee campaign (which has pledged to train 75 new beekeepers for London), the Co-operative's Plan Bee, the BBKA's Adopt a Beehive, and the National Trust's Bee Part Of It, are all aimed at supporting the honey bee, without whose pollination skills we would all be scuppered. And everyone can do their bit to convert their garden, allotment, balcony or window box into a bee-friendly glade by planting pollen rich trees, herbs and flowers, such as apples, plums, rosemary and thyme, sunflowers and foxgloves.

Trainee urban beekeeper Lynne Connell, Museum of London

A truly seasonal, local product, London honey comes on stream in late summer and autumn and is highly sought after, with different boroughs producing their own distinctive flavours and textures, from the dark runny 'Tate Honey', to the pale, lime scented honey made by bees 'working' the London parks. Borough Market, farmer's markets and select delis are a good source of London honey, as is Fortnum's, while Tate honey can be brought from the gallery's website. Reflecting the current buoyancy of the capital's beekeeping scene, the first London Honey Show was held in 2011 at the Lancaster London hotel (whose rooftop bees make the hotel's breakfast-time honey), with the Chelsea Physic Garden's deliciously floral honey (see p.56) carrying away several prizes.

Some Beekeeping Resources:

British Beekeepers Association
www.bbka.org.uk

London Beekeepers Association
www.lbka.org.uk

The Golden Company
www.thegoldenco-op.com

Pure Food
www.purefood.co.uk

Urban Bees
www.urbanbees.co.uk

The London Honey Company
www.thelondonhoneycompany.co.uk

Bees'n'Beans
www.beesnbeans.co.uk

Bees for Development
www.beesfordevelopment.org

Capital Bee
www.capitalbee.org.uk

Plan Bee
www.co-operative.coop

Bee part of it
www.nationaltrust.org.uk/beepartofit

Beehaus beehives
www.omlet.co.uk

The National Honey Show
www.honeyshow.co.uk

London Honey Show
www.londonbees.com

B   Beekeeping on RFH

Beehives don't come more stylish than the one tended by Mikey Tomkins and Barnaby Shaw on top of the Royal Festival Hall. The meticulous scale model of the iconic 1950s concert hall was built by sound artist Dr Robert Mullander using the original architects' drawings, and in 2008 the bees moved in.

The roof of the world-famous venue is a prestigious site but not necessarily the easiest one for the urban apiarist, with bees, honey and associated paraphernalia having to be carried through the Hall's main public spaces and up and down five floors. But a privileged view of the capital, across to the Houses of Parliament, St Paul's and down the Thames, makes up for it, along with the therapeutic effects of the bees themselves. According to Mikey, an enthusiastic practitioner and advocate for urban agriculture, beekeeping is a great lesson in learning to slow down and appreciate the complexity of things – 'no matter how hard one works at life, a colony of 50,000 female insects seems invariably better organised!'

Spring is a busy time for his charges as they prepare for their annual population explosion by collecting pollen and nectar. Throughout the summer Mikey and Barnaby look in on the three RFH hives once a week. The honey harvest usually takes place in August with the small but delicious yield (usually around 12-14 kg per hive) being sold at public and private events.

www.edibleurban.co.uk
www.royalfestivalhall.org.uk

> *Urban beekeeping feels like you're doing something despite all the best intentions of the city to deny you it. You discover that its hard concrete shells harbour a soft vegetative core and bees find this much quicker than we do."*

Bonnington Square Pleasure Garden

Named with a nod to the Vauxhall Pleasure Garden of old, this resident-run garden square may not have all the diversions offered by its famous forebear but what it lacks in orchestral performances, balloon flights, acrobats and masked balls it makes up in community spirit and charm. The site was developed in its current form in the mid 1990s, when residents successfully lobbied the council to save and redevelop the garden (at that point a derelict children's playground) for local people. Designed by 'committee', Bonnington Square's enclave of artistically inclined residents fortunately included garden designers Dan Pearson and James Frazer, who between them devised a luxuriant planting scheme, combining semi-tropical and Mediterranean plants with English natives.

The semi-tropical feel of the garden remains today, with lofty palms, Zealand flax, bananas, bamboos and mahonia providing the garden with its architecture and foliage. A small lawned area basks in the garden's sunlit centre, with benches for relaxing on, a picnic table and a children's play area among the amenities. Roped border edges and the odd anchor lying around add a faintly nautical feel to proceedings, while a giant iron slip wheel salvaged from a local marble works makes a dramatic sculptural contribution against the far wall. Such is the garden's exuberance that it has spilled out onto the Square's surrounding pavements, which have been planted with trees, shrubs and climbers as part of the Bonnington Square Garden Association's ongoing Paradise Project.

www.bonningtonsquaregarden.org.uk
www.bonningtoncafe.co.uk

Harleyford Road Community Garden

Begun in the 1980s, this community garden developed more organically than its neighbour, with no overriding design. As a result it is more jungle-like, with a relaxed feel compared to the orderly Bonnington Square. Here, winding mosaic pathways lead to several distinct areas, including a recently installed pond, children's play area, herb and vegetable beds, and a wildlife area (those nettles are there for a reason). Its 1.5 acres are gardened organically by regular volunteers, with the more experienced helping the less so, and its plants include well-established roses as well as more exotic specimens. Both gardens take part in the Open Garden Squares weekend (see p.170), with live music and a variety of stalls.

A 'secret' passage connects Bonnington Square with... Harleyford Road Community Garden

Rhododendrons, Cannizaro Park

C Cannizaro Park

What was once known as plain old Warren House acquired the altogether more exotic name of Cannizaro House when its then leaseholder inherited the Dukedom of Cannizaro in Sicily in 1832.

While the original 18th century mansion played host to the great and the good over the years (George III used to breakfast here after military reviews on Wimbledon Common), its residents were, when not entertaining, putting their stamp on the expansive gardens that roll out behind the house. Their efforts were not in vain – the 34 acre park is home to many unusual trees and shrubs and was designated a Grade II* listed garden of Historic Interest in 1987. Today the house is a privately owned luxury hotel but the park has been open to the public since 1949, having gone into council ownership in the previous year.

A cherished local resource, the park's lawns, woodlands and distinct garden spaces are a magnet for wildlife, picnickers and strollers (dogs are allowed on leads) and in the summer the area around the Italian Garden vibrates to the sounds of Cannizaro Festival.

Council run, albeit with energetic support from an active Friends organisation, Cannizaro still feels like a private garden, attractively scruffy in places and with a quirky variety of features – from the exuberant Millennium Fountain at the entrance to the gothic style aviary with its population of budgies. Notable statuary within the garden includes a bust of Haile Selassie, located in the Old Tennis Court area, commemorating the Ethiopian Emperor's exile in Wimbledon and a white marble depiction of the goddess Diana with a faun. Remnants of the garden's past can be glimpsed in Lady Jane's Wood, which was planted in 1793 by Viscount Melville to commemorate his marriage, and still forms part of the area known as the Azalea Dell. What is now the Italian Garden was once part of the Old Kitchen Garden, which provided the sociable household with fruit and veg.

Diana and Faun

Newer developments include the rustic style Water Garden, which was added in the post war period, and a herb garden, recently installed by the Friends. Cannizaro comes alive in the spring, when its lush camellias, magnolias, azaleas and rhododendrons erupt into flower – the colourful legacy of Kenneth and Adela Wilson, who owned Cannizaro between the two world wars and who lovingly restored the garden. They planted many of the rare trees and shrubs that Cannizaro is known for, choosing species such as camellia and rhododendrons, which relish the acid soil and free draining subsoil of the site. In spring the sunken garden near the hotel is jolly with serried ranks of tulips and spring flowers, while autumn colour doesn't disappoint either, courtesy of acers and maples, and other mature broad-leaved trees.

Set up in 1997 to help maintain the garden in the face of dwindling council budgets, the Friends actively care for and improve the gardens and have initiated major replanting in the Azalea Dell, Iris Beds and Water Garden. Some 80 new rhododrendrons were planted in the winter and spring of 2008-09.

Cannizaro Park
West Side Common, Wimbledon, SW19
www.merton.gov.uk www.cannizaropark.com
Open daily all year
Admission free

C Capel Manor Gardens

Cradled within the noisy embrace of the M25, just off junction 25, Capel Manor is a revelation, a thriving horticultural and animal husbandry college set in 30 acres of inspirational themed gardens. Visitor friendly features such as a restaurant and gift shop, and an animal corner stocked with cuddly alpacas, Shetland ponies and Kune Kune pigs make Capel Manor a great destination for family outings – even the family dog can join in the fun (as long as it's on a lead).

Like the Chelsea Flower Show, but without the irritating crowds and TV crews, Capel's imaginative show gardens are the main attraction, with a comprehensive array of different styles and themes to explore. Those with a historical bent should relish the nicely observed period features of the formal 17th-century style garden, the intricate Italianate maze, and the Victorian garden, with its serpentine lines, gazebo and colourful bedding schemes. To add a little perspective to these modern day interpretations it's worth remembering that the Capel Manor estate itself dates back to the 13th century, making the existing Georgian manor house virtually a new build in comparison.

For gardeners in search of inspiration there are plenty of practical garden layouts and ideas to filch – from a low allergen garden (planted entirely with insect-pollinated plants as opposed to high-allergy wind pollinated ones) to a security conscious family garden complete with a 'police approved' hedge. Of particular relevance to London based gardeners is the 'terraced house back garden' with its appealing sequence of well-defined spaces maximizing a typically long thin city plot.

The small gardens of 'Sunflower Street' showcase the talents of seven former Capel Manor College students with styles ranging from minimalist to Mediterranean, via a traditional blowsy cottage style garden. The College enjoys a deservedly high reputation, with graduates often going to enjoy glittering horticultural careers – pop-star cum gardening guru Kim Wilde is one such an alumna and her 'Jungle Gym Garden' here is great fun. Another creation by successful Capel graduates is 'Le Jardin de Vincent' – a beguiling evocation of a sun-soaked Provençal plot that won a medal at Chelsea Flower Show before being rebuilt on a larger scale at Capel.

As with all the best gardens, things don't stand still at Capel and new elements are regularly added. The Old Manor House Garden, with its ersatz 'Elizabethan' ruin, was opened in 2010 with a regal planting scheme celebrating Queens Elizabeth I and II, the latter monarch turning up in person to open the garden to the public. Bringing things up to date, this garden is bordered by a contemporary 'moat' – a state of the art natural swimming pond, which is enjoyed by Capel students on hot days. Other updated features include a redevelopment of the ½-acre Victorian Walled Garden to feature a display of 'instant gardening' as well as an ongoing collaboration between Capel Manor and Robert Mattock Roses that will establish the Walled Garden as home to a new historical collection of British bred traditional roses. Another gem here is the aromatic collection of scented pelargoniums in the greenhouse.

Maze

Old Manor House Garden

Trial beds

Hinduism

Faith Garden

Le Jardin de Vincent

The rear of the Walled Garden is earmarked for a display of modern and heritage fruit and veg. In the meantime, visitors with a taste for edible gardens are well-catered for elsewhere with the Thompson & Morgan fruit garden, experimental 'no-dig' vegetable plots, and trial gardens run by Gardening Which?.

More esoteric gardens include the meditative 'Growing Together in Faith' garden, which uses a rose motif to highlight the commonality of the four world religions. Built around a well-stocked koi pond, the Japanese Rock Garden offers an interpretation of eastern horticultural aesthetics while the Sensory Garden with its refreshing rill of running water, fragrant plants and easily accessible raised beds makes the point that gardening is for everybody. This philosophy is put into practice with hands-on workshops for physically disabled Enfield residents.

The gardens are divided into three areas for maintenance and with a ready supply of experience-hungry students it's perhaps no surprise to discover that Capel's grounds are beautifully tended, with an abundance of clearly labelled plants to ease identification. As befits a centre of learning, Capel holds several specific plant collections, including salvias, penstemons and the recently expanded National Collection of Sarcococcas. Students are set to work on key seasonal tasks like planting bedding, applying mulches and pruning roses.

Although sited at the London's outer limits, this 30-acre horticultural haven is well worth braving a trek across town and the somewhat lack lustre public transport links at the Enfield end. You may even find yourself signing up for a course…

Capel Manor College & Gardens
Bullsmoor Lane, Enfield, Middlesex, EN1 4RQ
www.capelmanorgardens.co.uk
T: 08456 122 122
See website for opening times and transport links

In a city where allotment spaces are rarer than the proverbial hens' teeth, Capital Growth has conjured and coaxed new veg-growing spaces out of the most unlikely places. Since its launch in November 2008, the project has helped to create hundreds of community food-growing plots across the city – on rooftops and in skips, on canal barges as well as in schools and housing estates.

A joint initiative between London Food Link, the Mayor of London, and the Big Lottery's Local Food Fund, the project aims to have created 2,012 food-growing spaces in London by the end of the Olympic year, 2012. Capital Growth puts its money where its mouth is and provides small grants to help groups who want to start or expand community food growing spaces, as well as offering training and support at centres across London (Regent's Park, NW1; Hammersmith Community Gardens Association Phoenix Farm, W12; Ravenscourt Park Greenhouses, W6; Growing Communities, Allen Gardens, N16; The London Wildlife Trust – Centre for Wildlife Gardening, Peckham, SE15). An offshoot project, Capital Bee, provides year-long training courses for fledgling community beekeepers at seven training sites across London (see Beekeeping Resources on p.25).

www.capitalgrowth.org

Growth grow-bags at Golden Lane Estate, see p.44

Ken Davies, Raquel Aquado, Melvyn Smith and Charlie

Capital Growth at Winterton House

Every time Melvyn Smith stepped out of his home at Winterton House, a refurbished 1960s tower block in Stepney, he was amazed by the unused piece of fenced off land that confronted him. 'The potential just smacked me in the face', he recalls and he set about applying for permission and funding to transform the run-down space into a community garden for the residents. Winterton House Organic Garden duly became Capital Growth's 533rd space and in February 2010 the land was cleared of its unkempt evergreen shrubs, its rubbish and its 100-strong rat population. A twenty-ton delivery of spent mushroom compost pepped up the exhausted soil and planting began in March, the garden having been divvied up into 14 small allotment spaces for residents and a communal garden, tended by volunteers. Just three months later the residents' hard work was rewarded when their garden won Best Newcomer and Best Community Garden & Allotment in Tower Hamlets in Bloom competition. The garden continues to develop, with veg-man Melvyn taking on a small flock of hens and ducks, and his friend 'the flower genius' Ken Davis planting a magnificent alpine bed in a tricky, exposed part of the site.

For residents of Winterton House, the garden has turned out to be a real icebreaker and a great way of neighbours getting to know each other. Like gardeners everywhere, tips are offered, help given and produce swapped. For allotment holders Derek and Billy the garden has been a positive development, 'Billy and I are widowers and its put another dimension in our lives. There are bonuses already – it's been years since I had a suntan and people say to me 'you look so healthy, have you been away?'

www.captitalgrowth.org
www.opensquares.org

Billy Vaughan and Derek Thompson

"Just by transforming our environment we've also transformed our whole community. Its made people come together, it's made people talk to each other."

Barbara & Boris

Kodu gourd

42

Capital Growth & Rocky Park Growers

Gardening has enhanced the lives of residents at the Hollybush and Teesdale Estate in more ways than one. The vegetable gardens that have been installed on once vacant and vandalised patches of land on the Estate have not only introduced residents to the joy of growing-your-own, and improved the view from their flats, but they've also helped to foster a sense of community and reduce anti-social behaviour.

The brainchild of Margaret Cox, chair of the Estate's Tenants' and Residents' Association, the Urban Growers project began in April 2009 with 15 raised beds installed in Rocky Park – a disused children's play area. This proved such a hit that other fallow spaces around the estate were quickly commandeered to quadruple the number of beds available to residents. In response to feedback from growers, the beds now have built-in frames for growing climbing produce such as kodu gourds, a favourite Bangladeshi crop. Spaces that were once a magnet for drug dealers and noisy late night ball games are now respected and enjoyed by the whole community, with seats and communal herb beds for all to use.

An entirely voluntary, resident-led organization, the Urban Growers rely on good will and enthusiasm. Loyal bands of corporate volunteers (many from the Financial Services Authority) have helped to build much of the garden's infrastructure. According to Rocky Park volunteer and RTA secretary, Sarah Beydoun, they get as much out of their work as the residents do, 'They really care about what they're doing here – they really like to see the positive impact they are having on the community and they return time and time again'.

With a raft of awards to their name, the Urban Growers are forging ahead. They have already planted an urban orchard – the first in Tower Hamlets – and future plans include a greenhouse, an eco classroom and communal raspberry canes. With help from Capital Growth, the Urban Growers have also set up a grow-to-sell scheme, selling organically grown crops to a local restaurant, with proceeds being reinvested in the project.

Rocky Park Urban Growers
Ellsworth Street, Tower Hamlets, E2 0AX

Capital Growth at Golden Lane

The residents of Golden Lane Estate have got container gardening down to a fine art – even their allotments are containerised, with each plot comprising a compost-filled builders' bag resting on a wooden pallet. Container growing is a fact of life on the Grade II listed estate (the older sibling of the nearby Barbican Estate and likewise designed by architects, Chamberlain, Powell and Bon), since even its concrete landscaping is protected by its listed status.

Over the decades since Golden Lane's completion in 1962 its residents have become adept at 'gardening on concrete', learning to tailor their plant choices around the broiling sunspots and ferocious cross winds generated by the estate's topography. Gardeners here report big differences between what will grow on the ground level gardens of the terrace blocks and what is able to thrive on the high-rise balconies of Great Arthur House, the 16-storey tower that was once England's highest block of flats. Geraniums are Nicholas Lee's first choice for his balcony – 'they're mega-boring but they are the only things that survive! And they don't seem to attract any bugs either, which is good.' Elsewhere on the estate fragrant jasmine is popular, while at outside her flat at Bayer House, Liz Davis has created a mini woodland with oak, rowan, plum and birch trees – 'I love trees, I try to make it like a forest'. At Basterfield House, Bev Bytheway mixes mature architectural plants inherited from her predecessor with informal seasonal planting and she is collaborating with her neighbours to see how they can improve habitats for birds and insects.

It's a sociable place to be a gardener, with plants often exchanged amongst neighbours and an active gardening forum on the Estate's website. The allotments are the logical extension of this community spirit but are a relatively new development having been set up in 2010 on an empty patch of ground outside Basterfield House with funding from Capital Growth and the City of London. The initial 20 'plots' have subsequently grown to around 31 plots looked after by around 50 'baggers'; prior gardening knowledge is not necessary as the Golden Lane Garden club runs a 'buddy' scheme whereby experienced gardeners help out those with less know-how.

Golden Lane Estate, EC1Y 0TN

C Carlyle's House

Clocking in at just 79 x 20 feet, this is a historic garden on a scale that most of us can relate to. Tucked away behind an early 18th century terraced house, the garden's claim to fame is that it was once tended by Victorian 'celebrity' literary couple Jane and Thomas Carlyle. They moved into 24 Cheyne Row in 1834, spending the rest of their married lives here.

Back in those days, Chelsea was not the pukka postcode it is today and the house provided affordable accommodation, where the 'sage of Chelsea' penned his epic and today largely unread historical studies, and the couple received the leading artists and writers of the day.

The marriage was not the most straightforward or happiest of unions but both Jane and Thomas shared a passion for their modest back garden. Responsibilities divided along traditional gender lines: Thomas was keen on vegetable growing and buying tools while Jane was in charge of flowers and nurturing, often introducing cuttings and plants from her native Scotland. One mystery seedling she transplanted turned out to be a gooseberry, another a nettle; their lowly horticultural status did not deter Jane from fussing over them like sickly children.

The couple's letters and journals reveal an ongoing devotion to what they called their 'gardenkin' and both worked enthusiastically to transform the barren patch. Their frustrations and preoccupations are familiar to anyone gardening today –bizarre weather patterns, unresponsive plants, overzealous hired help, and frantic garden tidy ups before the arrival of visitors. Although Jane lamented that 'Mr C. does not know a myrtle from a nettle', Thomas enjoyed gardening and also liked escaping to the garden to enjoy a quiet smoke. Carlyle was fond of writing in the garden – setting up his table on the lawn, beneath an awning which, pictured in photographs of the time, looks for all the world like the 'sails' favoured by modern garden designers.

Today the garden is tended by custodian Lin Skippings, with additional help from Linda Chinnery and one other volunteer. The present layout was planned by Anthony Lord in 1980 and includes many features that would have been familiar to the Carlyle's – such as the box edged borders enclosing the fig and pear tree by the privy, and the rectangular patch of lawn with gravel path skirting around it. Linda and her team garden in the spirit of the Carlyle's rather than being strictly historically accurate. A vine and the all important gooseberry have been reintroduced, while the recent loss of an overbearing walnut tree in the far corner has opened up light and space for a veg patch. In keeping with Mrs Carlyle's fondness for plants with sentimental attachment, Linda has also added bluebells, aquilegia and even a nettle from Jane's childhood garden in Scotland. Also in keeping with historical accuracy is Lin's microscopic budget – a shade over £100 for the year at the time of writing – visitors who bring cuttings and seeds are welcomed!

The borders are probably a little fuller and prettier than they were in the Carlyle's day – the shady border that runs alongside the lawn features popular Victorian plants like ferns and laurel as well as Geranium phaeum and climbing hydrangea while on the sunny border opposite a pink rose winds through a trellis. Lighting up the shade beneath the pear tree are woodland stalwarts like diacentra, foxglove, and pulmonaria. In late spring deep pink peonies and purple lilac, bloom against the warmth of the far wall. Being walled and near the river, the garden enjoys a warm microclimate but unlike many walled gardens it doesn't – according to Linda – suffer too badly with slugs and snails, which is probably just as well since the garden is run as organically as possible.

Carlyle's House
24 Cheyne Row, SW3 5HL
www.nationaltrust.org.uk
T: 020 7352 7087
Open: Wed-Sun 11.00-17.00 (Mar-Oct)

Carlyle's House Garden

C Centre for Wildlife Gardening

Proving that cities and the natural world need not be mutually exclusive, the CfWG leads by example, its 0.25ha site in downtown Peckham burgeons with great ideas for boosting urban biodiversity.

Its collection of demonstration mini-habitats shows that the urban jungle can also be home to wildflower meadows, woodland copses, mini-beast villages, as well as more traditional ornamental gardens. Taking advantage of these tailor-made environments on their door-step are songbirds, birds of prey, foxes, endangered invertebrates like stag beetles (for whom London is something of a stronghold), as well as picnicking mums and their hungry broods. Reinstalled here after its gold medal winning debut at Hampton Court Flower Show in 2009, the 'future garden' inspires gardeners to rise to the challenge of climate change with its bold use of recycled materials and drought resistant planting scheme incorporating toughies likes sedum and teasel.

The site is a productive one too – vegetables are grown year-round in a cluster of sturdy wooden raised beds while two beehives produce 'Peckham Honey' that is much in demand with local hay fever sufferers. Various community groups grow flowers and veg here, including the 'Happy Flowers', a long-standing group of gardeners with learning disabilities, and the 'Sweet Peas', a green fingered group of pensioners. Plants and seed raised on the site can be purchased for modest sums from the on-site nursery and come with useful information about each plant's wildlife garden credentials.

A hard-working educational resource, the Centre is popular with schools groups and offers hands-on activities like pond-dipping, dragonfly spotting, mini-beast hunts as well as a 'frog day' in late March. The friendly team of volunteers who help run the garden also benefit from a structured programme of on-site training and happily pass their knowledge on to visitors, dispensing tips about how to achieve a chemical free, wildlife garden (including how to deter the wildlife you *don't* want). Got a slug problem? Try putting down used coffee grounds to deter the little blighters. And as for unwanted foxes, lion dung is apparently the answer. Keeping your soil in good heart is crucial if you want to garden organically and if you're unsure about how to convert your kitchen and garden waste into compost, there's a comparative display of bins to help make your mind up – from no-nonsense 'Daleks' to state of the art wormeries, which are ideal for small garden households.

At the hub of all this activity is the centre's funky, award-winning visitor centre, which sports an expansive 'living roof', and houses a classroom-cum-meeting space and the London Wildlife Trust's Southwark office. The centre is also furnished with some aesthetically pleasing art works, including bollards by Antony Gormley and a pair of intricate, wildlife themed wrought iron entrance gates by Heather Burrell.

Centre for Wildlife Gardening
28 Marsden Road, SE15 4EE
www.wildlondon.org.uk
T: 020 7252 9186

C Chelsea Flower Show

For some it's the first cuckoo, for others it's the evenings drawing out but for many the real harbinger of summer is the Chelsea Flower Show. Every May this well-heeled corner of London goes gardening mad as the RHS's premier show takes over the grounds of the Royal Hospital, transforming them beyond recognition with stunning 'instant' gardens, floral marquees and retail opportunities by the barrow load. Even the shops on Sloane Street and the King's Road get into the spirit of things with extravagant floral themed store fronts.

The show gardens and the famous Floral Pavilion are the big crowd pleasers here, showcasing the skills of designers and plants people from Britain and around the world. The horticultural equivalent of an haute couture catwalk, Chelsea is the place to spot the hottest trends, from eco-chic to vertical planting, before they filter down to the mass market.

The show gardens are the work of some of the biggest names in international garden design and the mega-bucks fantasy gardens they create for Chelsea seem to spring up as if from nowhere, belying months, if not years, of preparation. Incredibly, most of them look as if they've been in-situ forever. Newly introduced in 2012, the Fresh show garden category replaced the Urban Gardens of previous years and promises innovative, cutting edge gardens, with designers being freed from some of Chelsea's usual judging restrictions. By contrast, the **Artisan Garden** category puts the emphasis on natural, sustainably sourced materials and traditional craftsmanship.

Whatever the category of show garden (and these are subject to change from time to time), the free planting plans that are dished out at every turn are worth picking up for their take home design ideas and plant lists. And for those whose idea of gardening is more spectator than contact sport, there are always of plenty of inviting 'garden structures', from humble shed to trendy 'pod'.

Heavily covered on television by the BBC, Chelsea is insanely popular – be prepared to wade your way through heavy crowds with a holiday atmosphere. Some 157,000 visitors come to the CFS every year – and expect to queue, or stand on tip-toe, to see some exhibits. Like the Wimbledon tennis tournament, you probably actually get to see more of the show gardens on the box than you do in real life, but it's a different story inside the Great Pavilion. This wonderfully scented arena is

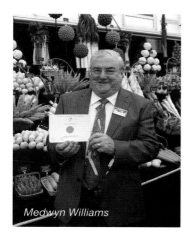
Medwyn Williams

Garden designer Diarmuid Gavin

Garden designer Andy Sturgeon

Garden designer Joe Swift

the place to admire expertly staged plants at close quarters, many of them blooming unseasonably early, and to meet some of the nurserymen and women who coax perfection from flora as various as pelargoniums, dahlias, sweet peas and roses. Some well-known nurseries such as Kelways, Notcutts and Avon Bulbs have been coming to Chelsea for years and the floral pavilion is a testament to their horticultural prowess. Exhibitors are usually very approachable and happy to answer questions. The talent is not all home-grown, and displays from further afield – the Cayman Islands, Bermuda, South Africa – overflow with exotic plants. Here, as with the show gardens, exhibitors vie with each other for a coveted RHS medal (either bronze, silver, silver-gilt or gold), awarded by a panel of eagle-eyed judges.

Although on a smaller scale to the Great Pavilion, the Floral Design Marquee can be an equally intense experience. Over 150 NAFAS (National Association of Flower Arranging Societies), individuals and groups compete to create the ultimate floral arrangement. The resulting inventive, intricate floral creations are always worth seeing, as the queues suggest, and are likely to make those whose normal approach to floristry is plonking a bunch of blooms in a vase of water feel rather inadequate.

Retail opportunities, needless to say, are never far away. If you haven't blown the budget on a Pimms and a sandwich (quite possible at Chelsea), then head for the stalls ranged in the shade of the London plane trees on Eastern Avenue. This is your opportunity to stock up on all manner of goodies, from upmarket gardening attire to the latest pruning gizmo or all singing and dancing water features, or even a work of art. The legendary plant sell-off at the end of the last day has something of the Harrods' sale about it, but there are some amazing specimens to be had if you can beat off the competition and find a way to transport your prize home safely.

Chelsea Flower Show Royal Hospital Road, SW3
www.rhs.org.uk

C Chelsea Fringe

A gardening festival started in 2011 by garden journalist and writer Tim Richardson, the Chelsea Fringe unleashes a mix of horticultural happenings at venues across London for three weeks in May.

Although the Fringe coincides with the RHS Chelsea Flower Show and operates with its support, it is completely independent, and in its organisers' words, promises to 'explode out of the show ground geographically, demographically and conceptually'.

Not-for-profit and volunteer run, the Fringe is entirely in the spirit of the contemporary gardening scene in London, with an open access principle that embraces everything from grass roots community garden projects to avant-garde art installations, and work by horticultural professionals as well as enthusiasts.

www.chelseafringe.com

Dalston Curve Garden

Floating Garden,
City Road Basin

Pothole Gardener

Meadow up your street

David Harber, Sundial

Hogarth Roundabout

Edible bus stop

Order Beds, Chelsea Physic Garden

London's historic gardens don't come more venerable than this, the Chelsea Physic Garden. Occupying a 3.8 acre site of prime Chelsea riverside, the CPG has been cultivating plants here since its foundation in 1673, when the Society of Apothecaries needed somewhere handy to park their state barge and a place where they could grow and study medicinal plants.

Today, this jewel of a botanic garden remains a centre for horticultural research and conservation as well as a living showcase for the amazing medicinal resource that is the plant world. It's a great place to unwind too – a gentle stroll around its tranquil paths and themed planted areas makes the perfect counterpoint to a hectic shopping spree on the King's Road.

With over 300 years of experience behind them, the CPG effortlessly combines beauty with educational purpose. The Garden of World Medicine is an ethnobotanic display of medicinal plants used by different cultures, from the *Cordyline australis* of the Maoris and the *Ocimum tenuiflorum* of the Ayurvedic tradition to the *Gingko biloba* of traditional Chinese medicine. In contrast to these beds (where not all the plants here have been scientifically proven), the nearby Pharmaceutical Beds are filled with plants of proven value in current medicinal practice. Arranged by branch of medicine, they reveal how reliant we are on seemingly everyday plants such as yew and barley in disciplines as diverse as oncology and anaesthesia. If only there were a remedy for mankind's tendency to exploit to extinction – the CPG conserves medicinal plants such as blue cohosh and bloodroot that are now endangered thanks to over-enthusiastic harvesting. The latest development at the garden, the new Garden of Edible and Useful Plants, gloriously shows the extent to which we rely on plants for every aspect of our lives: from foods to building materials, clothing and cleaning to arts and ritual. It includes an intriguing and beautiful amphitheatre of plants used in perfumery and aromatherapy, including the gorgeously scented *Pelargonium odoratissimum* (Geranium), and *Rosa centifolia*, the source of attar of roses.

Statue of Sir Hans Soane

The presence of systematic order beds reminds us that the CPG is a proper botanic garden; divided between monocotyledons and dicotyledons, these beds are designed to show the botanical relationship between plants. It is fascinating to find out where plants originate – *Alchemilla speciosa* from the Caucasus, *Camassia quamash* from western North America. To the south of the garden Fortune's Tank Pond is a focus for the CPG's teeming wildlife – water boatmen, damselflies, newts and leeches. During the summer it is surrounded by a mini wildflower meadow of British native species such as *Centaurea cyanus* (cornflower) – and a popular port of call with the Garden's bee population. Their hives can be seen in the Mediterranean woodland area and the honey can be purchased in the shop.

Over on the western side of the garden, the Historical Walk tells the story of the CPG through the plants introduced by some of its key players. This amounts to a roll call of some of the biggest names in gardening history, including explorer and naturalist Sir Joseph Banks, William Forsyth (who

of the Tropical Corridor house spectacular south American orchids and tender rarities such as *Brighamia insignis*, a native of Hawaii. Fashioned from an unlikely combination of Icelandic lava and stone from the Tower of London, the 18th-century rock garden is possibly the earliest of its kind in Europe and is the backdrop to a collection of Cretan plants including *Petromarula pinnata* (Wall Lettuce).

With a garden of this scope, a single visit will not be enough. Seasonal changes make it a garden to return to time and again – from bud burst to leaf drop. The serried ranks of specimens displayed in the old-fashioned plant 'theatre' encapsulate this progression with plants as diverse as snow drops and chillies, depending on the time of year. Annual membership buys various privileges, chief amongst them year-round access to the garden (the general public are usually only allowed in April-October). And although children are limited to two per accompanying adult, there's plenty for budding young gardeners to enjoy within the CPG walls, with points of interest including sinister-looking carnivorous plants, mysterious mandrakes and delicious dinosaur fodder in the Cool Fernery. Lectures and the ever-popular compost clinics offer more grown-up appeal but the CPG is not all about education – there are leisure opportunities aplenty. On warm summer days the lawn is filled with languid, Chelsea picnickers while the in-house café serves top-notch home-cooked light lunches and teas whatever the weather. The well-stocked shop is full of nice smells and gardening goodies – seeds, soaps, plants and preserves, as well as the odd useful implement.

name to Forsythia) and the 19th century plant hunter Robert Fortune, who introduced tea production to India from China. A statue of another major figure in the CPG is given pride of place, slap bang in the centre of the garden – Sir Hans Sloane (1660-1753), the great physician, scientist and collector. Sloane ensured the survival of the CPG when he granted the Apothecaries a lease on the site for an annual rent of £5 – on the proviso that the garden was kept in perpetuity as a 'physic garden'. The peppercorn rent is still paid to his descendants. Sloane's collections went on to form the basis of the British Museum and later the Natural History Museum, but he is also remembered (with gratitude) for bringing the first recipe for milk chocolate to these shores.

Blessed with a free draining soil that most London gardeners can only dream of, a southerly aspect and a balmy microclimate, the garden is home to many unusual, tender and endangered species. The largest outdoor grown olive tree in Britain is found here, while the beds just inside the Swan Walk entrance are devoted to tender plants from the Canary Islands, such as the rare *Echium wildpretii*, whose native habitat is atop a volcano in Tenerife. Protected by a fleece in winter, this exotic border really kicks off in June, when the 8ft blue flower spikes of *Echium pinniana* are in full bloom. Glasshouses have been a feature of the garden since its earliest days, and today the greenhouses

The Chelsea Physic Garden
Swan Walk, SW3 4HS
www.chelseaphysicgarden.co.uk
T: 020 7352 5646
Open: 1 April-30 October;
Tues, Wed, Thurs & Fri 12noon-17.00;
Sun & Public Holidays 12noon-18.00;
Special late night opening on Weds in July & August until 22.00

A view of The Exedra taken from inside Chiswick House

Popular with local dog walkers (who even have their own association, the wittily named CHOW), the gardens of Chiswick House are also revered as the birthplace of the English Landscape Garden. It was here in the 1720's and 30's that, working alongside the architect-owner of Chiswick House Lord Burlington, William Kent pioneered the 'picturesque' garden, creating playful, Arcadian vistas after the manner of Poussin and Claude's landscape paintings. Although subsequent residents of Lord Burlington's neo-Palladian villa also put their stamp on the terrain, many of Kent and Burlington's innovations have survived and are looking better than they have for a long while, thanks to a multi-million pound restoration completed in 2010.

Classical references abound: Kent and Burlington had met on the Grand Tour and enthusiastically set about recreating what they had seen in Italy at Chiswick. A Doric column (today surmounted by a freshly carved Venus de Medici) rises majestically from the rose garden, an equally emphatic obelisk spikes the circular pond at the heart of the Orange Tree Garden, itself overseen by a dinky Ionic temple. The Exedra, a semi-circular yew hedge at the rear of the house, is punctuated with niches filled with statesman-like Roman statues and classical urns, while strategically placed sphinxes and lions patrol the area like latter day guard dogs.

Burlington looked to ancient Roman precedent in the garden's layout too, using a device known as a 'patte d'oie' (goose-foot) to create trios of avenues radiating out from a central hub, each spoke terminating in an eye-catching feature such as the quaint Rustic House. Renaissance gardens provided the inspiration for the Cascade, Burlington's last major work at Chiswick. This tumbling waterfall, at one end of the serpentine River, never worked properly in Burlington's time but modern technology has finally overcome the centuries' old teething problems and today water gushes dramatically down the rocky descent. The graceful balustraded stone bridge which arches over the River is actually a canalised

stream, formerly known as the Bollo Brook. It post-dates Burlington's time, having been installed by the 5th Duke of Devonshire in 1774, but is a perfect focal point, forming the shared terminus of two interlinking patte d'oies.

One of the most mutable art forms, gardens by their very nature never stand still. Luckily for us Lord Burlington was so proud of his creation at Chiswick that he commissioned a set of 8 paintings by Pieter Rysbrack. These views – reunited finally after their dispersal in the 1950s – are displayed inside the house and offer a fascinating picture of Kent and Burlington's gardens in the early 18th century, with their painterly arrangements of allées, woodland and classical ornament. A major resource for the restoration team, the paintings also record features that have been lost, including various garden buildings designed by Burlington and the estate's original Jacobean manor house.

Despite their historic significance, the gardens slid into a decline in the 20th century, having become a much loved but rather neglected public park in the late 1920s. Ever dwindling local authority budgets meant that whilst hedges and lawns were cut, Chiswick's carefully designed woodland glades grew dense with self-sown trees and shrubs, Kent's artful vistas became distorted and the footfall of over 1 million visitors a year took its toll on pathways and lawns. In 2005 the independent Chiswick House and Gardens Trust was set up to oversee the £12.1 million restoration, which would respect the key elements of Kent and Burlington's work whilst embracing the wider history of the gardens and their contemporary role as a recreational space for locals and visitors.

Today the gardens are well on the way to recovery. A campaign of tree felling has been balanced by the planting of new specimens in areas such as the Grove, the Northern Wilderness and the Camellia Shrubbery. The Western Lawn – now liberated from its municipal clutter of rubbish bins, railings and random benches – once again sweeps expansively down from the house to the river, roses bloom in the Rosary as they did in the 19th century, and the famous octet of Cedars of Lebanon in the forecourt have been renewed with young specimens, propagated from the surviving originals.

Once deemed unsafe for the general public, the Grade I listed Conservatory – designed by Samuel Ware for the 6th Duke of Devonshire in 1813 – has been comprehensively repaired and conserved. Its historic and rare collection of camellias is celebrated in an annual Camellia Festival, launched in 2011. A precursor of the great glass structures of Kew and Chatsworth, the Conservatory has a further claim to fame in being one of the locations (along with the Exedra) used in the Beatles 1966 'Paperback Writer' pop promo. The 96 metre long glass structure looks out over the manicured, geometric flower-beds of the Italian Garden, which was laid out in 1812 by Lewis Kennedy and has likewise been restored to its Regency pomp.

The walled garden that lies behind the Conservatory originally served as the kitchen garden to nearby Moreton Hall and was purchased by the 6th Duke in 1812. Now once again operating as a productive space for fruit and vegetable growing, it is used for community gardening projects and is open to the public on selected days.

Thankfully, the unique ambience of the house and garden has survived the restoration. Built as a party

The restored rosary & Doric column, Chiswick House

pad-cum-art gallery by Lord Burlington, Chiswick House has been the scene of some memorable parties over the centuries, hosting Tsars, Shahs and any number of British royals and aristos, and it is still a fun place to visit. The laid-back atmosphere can best be absorbed over coffee and cake in the award-winning café designed by Caruso St John; energetic youngsters can burn off excess energy in the adjacent play area while their elders can conserve theirs in comfort. A dog-friendly destination since Lord B's day, the garden features all manner of pooches on parade and hosts a popular annual dog show, complete with celebrity judges. If the season and weather permit, visitors might want to watch a cricket match, play a game of tennis, catch an outdoor movie screening or perhaps enjoy a picnic on the refurbished (dog-free) Wilderness Lawn.

Writing to Lord Burlington in 1731, apropos of his architectural interests and projects, the poet Alexander Pope advised the earl to 'Consult the genius of the place in all'. Like Kent and Burlington before them, the restoration team at Chiswick have clearly taken this advice to heart and their work here has triumphantly revived one of Britain's most iconic gardens, whilst sympathetically equipping it for the demands of a 21st century public.

Chiswick House, Burlington Lane, W4 2RP
www.chgt.org.uk · T: 020 8995 0508
Open: April, Daily 10.00-17.00;
May-Oct Sun-Wed & Public Holidays 10.00-17.00
Admission Charge

C City Gardens

There's more to the City than fat cat bankers and shiny office blocks. Built up as it is, the Square Mile is also home to a quirky collection of gardens, planted highways, churchyards and burial grounds.

Although most of the gardens themselves are post WWII creations, history is unavoidable in London's most ancient quarter, with sites incorporating everything from Roman remains to plague pits alongside the latest in contemporary architecture.

Most of the City's 200 open spaces are managed by the Corporation of London, with biodiversity high on the agenda. Wildlife friendly initiatives include insect hotels, bird and bat boxes, green roofs, nectar rich planting, and the use of pheromone traps instead of chemical pesticides. The Corporation's Department of Open Spaces uses peat-free bedding medium in its planters, as well as raising some 250,000 bedding plants in its own nursery in West Ham Park – thus reducing plant miles. It's a strategy that seems to be working because in recent years the City has become a habitat for rare species such as the Peregrine Falcon and is a stronghold for the country's Black Redstart population. The Barbican Estate is home to a healthy population of the once common but now endangered house sparrow while strategically placed log piles have been created in gardens such as Finsbury Circus, in the hope of enticing stag beetles into the City.

City gardens flourish in the face of considerable adversity. The air is polluted and the soil is poor, compacted and of limited depth – beneath its scanty surface runs a Swiss cheese labyrinth of communications cables, power lines, sewers, railway lines, cellars and basements, not to mention burial sites and archaeological remains. Although there's a toasty microclimate that favours exotic species, some native plants resent the generally

dry conditions, while the City's tall buildings create destructive wind tunnels and vortexes. The relentless redevelopment of the City (one third in the past 30 years) causes its own problems too, particularly for trees, which need time to mature and which are susceptible to damage or removal by reckless contractors.

But its not all doom and gloom; over the past 30 years the number of green spaces in the City has increased tenfold as all new building developments have to show an environmental gain. It also helps that the City's open spaces are protected by their own Acts of Parliament and that over £1.5 million a year is lavished on their upkeep (although much of this goes on staff wages for the team of 35 gardeners who look after the City gardens, and this amount is likely to decrease in the future due to budget cuts). A walk around the City quickly confirms that its well-used and much loved gardens are as much a part of its identity as chalk stripe suits, and telephone number salaries.

This page: Lakeside Terrace, Barbican

Carter Lane Gardens

Carter Lane Gardens

Hard by the funky folded-metal structure that is the City Information Centre, Carter Lane Gardens makes a good start point for a garden themed walk through the City of London. The gardens were re-landscaped in 2009 with an eco-minded scheme of orderly evergreen hedges, accompanied by swathes of bee-friendly and drought tolerant lavender and *Gaura lindheimeri*. With benches and closely cropped lawns for lounging on, it's tempting to linger, but other treasures await...

St Paul's Churchyard

St Paul's Churchyard

The garden here was first laid out as an Open Space in 1878 and combines the burial grounds of the various churches that have occupied this area over the centuries (St Paul's, St Gregory by St Paul's and St Faith the Virgin under St Paul's). Today the garden comprises a formal rose garden, planted in 1976, grassed areas and mature trees, with benches and a few venerable tombs. This being St Paul's Cathedral the garden hardware is a cut above, and includes rare early 18th-century iron railings, the 19th-century St Paul's Cross, a memorial to Londoners killed in WWII. The statue of John Wesley is always accompanied by a red and white planting scheme, the traditional colours of the Methodist movement. The tree population features a weeping mulberry in the North garden, two *Gingko biloba* trees and several walnut trees (with attendant squirrels).

Festival Gardens

Festival Gardens

Built on the site of the 13th century thoroughfare, Old Change, this formal sunken garden was designed by the classically inclined architect Sir Albert Richardson to celebrate the 1951 Festival of Britain. Like so many City gardens it occupied land cleared courtesy of the Luftwaffe ten years previously and the garden follows the footprint of the Livery Hall that stood on the site until 1941. The garden is enclosed on three sides by pleached limes and has recently been renovated – its Portland stone fountain scrubbed clean and its newly laid lawn made fully accessible to the public for the first time with additional benches also part of the new spec.

22 Cannon Street Garden

Although you would never guess it, this elegant ½ acre garden sits atop an underground car park and is officially classed as a roof garden. Its central space is a crisp oval lawn, smartly mown with business-like stripes, which is offset by a predominantly green and white planting scheme in the surrounding borders. Good use is made of foliage plants such as fatsia, magnolia and rhododendrons, which are underplanted with numerous bulbs and lilies of the valley.

Cleary Garden

This hillside garden has a rich history having been a Roman bathhouse, a piggery, a medieval vineyard and a newspaper print works. In 1940 the latter was destroyed, and the resulting bomb site was gardened by Joseph Brandis, a shoemaker, who used mud from the Thames and soil and plants from his home in Walthamstow to effect the garden's transformation.

A visit from the then Queen in 1949, and its position above a section of the District Line, assured the makeshift garden's survival. In 1982 it was comprehensively redesigned to commemorate the centenary of the Metropolitan Parks and Gardens Association and named in honour of one of the Association's movers and shakers, Fred Cleary. Following a further overhaul in 2007 the garden has returned to its vintner's roots, with the addition of vines from the Loire Valley. Arranged over three levels the garden descends, via a sturdy brick and timber pergola to a lawn, beneath which lie the remains of the Roman baths. The pergola is festooned with roses, wisteria and clematis and on street level is accompanied by a bed of peonies, gifted by the Shimane prefecture in Japan. The planting is beefed up by some fabulous trees, including *Taxodium ascendens* (pond cypress), *Metasequoia glyptostroboides* (dawn redwood) and the drought-loving *Pinus strobus* (eastern white pine). Benches cater for human visitors while an insect hotel and bird boxes help the City's wildlife.

22 Cannon Street Garden

Cleary Garden

Christchurch Greyfriars Garden

Postman's Park

Christchurch Greyfriars Garden

This pretty garden, laid out within the walls of a ruined Wren church (itself built on the site of the medieval Franciscan church of Greyfriars) has recently been replanted as a cottage garden, although some roses from its previous incarnation as a rosary remain. The ten wooden towers, home to adventuresome clematis and assorted bird boxes, represent the pillars of the nave whose footings can still be glimpsed amongst the wildlife friendly mounds of gaura, ladies' mantle, agapanthus, heuchera, geranium and catmint. Although reputedly haunted by two highborn murderesses, the site is relatively tranquil today, with visitors more likely to be disturbed by passing traffic than any paranormal activity.

Postman's Park

Not quite the 'hidden London' find it once was, thanks to the film of Patrick Marber's *Closer*, but a historic and interesting City garden nonetheless. The site became a public garden in 1880 and was much beloved of local postal workers but, as the gravestones dotted about suggest, it was once a churchyard. The tiled panels of the memorial wall by GF Watts record heart-rending acts of bravery by ordinary people, the latest addition dates from 2007. Being dark and shady it's a difficult spot to garden, but an eclectic collection of plants thrives here, including tree ferns and bananas and the City's only publically accessible horse chestnut tree. Seasonal highlights are delivered by snakes head fritillaries, Japanese anemones and, in June, the dazzling white bracts of the handkerchief tree, *Davidia involucrata*.

St Mary Staining

A simply laid out garden sited on a former burial ground and surrounded on three sides by buildings by the 'big three' of contemporary British architecture: Richard Rogers, Nicholas Grimshaw and Norman Forster. The curving and sloping façade of the latter's building is a result of the architect having to accommodate an existing plane tree, protected by a preservation order.

Monkwell Square

Part of the surrounding development, designed by Terry Farrell in the 1980s, this small garden has a strong personality. Essentially a large brick and stone raised bed, with matching balusters and stone obelisks, it is boldly planted with mop head, broad leaf trees in each corner, and a double avenue of yew topiary cones with a strip of lawn at either side. A number of "Flowers in the City" plaques attest to its popularity.

St Alphage Garden & St Alphage Garden Podium

The rather basic lawn, hedge and benches arrangement of St Alphage is given a little extra glamour by a huge Magnolia kobus and the fact that it shares a section of the Roman wall with the Salters' Garden (see p.146). At the far end, steps lead down to a lower level with raised beds, planted with a different bedding scheme each year. From here a gate gives access into the Salters' Garden.

Things get more exciting up on the Highwalk, a roof garden with real panache. Here a prairie style planting of grasses is enlivened by seasonal drifts of colour from alliums, sisyrinchium and hellebores, with backbone provided by wind resistant toughies like elaeagnus and choisya. Michael Ayrton's Minotaur sculpture broods amid the greenery, having been relocated here from Postman's Park in 1997

Highwalk, St Alphage Garden

Aldermanbury Square

Not really a garden, but its cool, contemporary use of trees, grasses and hard landscaping is worth a look. The current layout dates from 2006, when traffic was excluded from the square. It features a grove of 14 hugely expensive 'table-pruned' London planes along one side, beneath which bubble water features placed in the sleek granite paving. On the opposite side, silver birch trees are under-planted with alliums and grasses, whose seeds provide food for birds. Part-funded by a nearby development project, the square exudes quality, right down to its stylish scattering of wooden chairs and its memorial to the Millennium, a standing stone inscribed by David Kindersley.

St Lawrence Jewry

Brewers' Hall Garden

Just off Aldermanbury Square, this street-side garden consists of three brick built raised beds, planted with resilient perennials like ladies' mantle, bergenia and periwinkle and evergreen shrubs such as sarcococca. A statue by Karin Jonzen depicting a gardener at work illustrates why bad backs and knees are a common complaint among horticulturalists.

St Mary Aldermanbury

A peaceful garden with three distinct areas, standing on the former site of the church and churchyard of the same name. The Wren church, which replaced a 15th-century predecessor, was damaged in the Blitz and subsequently relocated to Fulton, Missouri as a memorial to Winston Churchill (he made his famous 'Iron Curtain' speech in Fulton). In return for the church, Fulton gave the garden the swamp cypress at the far end of the garden.

Remnants of the medieval church remain within the garden, and the lawn is studded with the footings of the columns that once defined the nave. The church has no shortage of historical associations – infamous Judge Jefferies was buried here, and it was in this parish that John Hemynge and Henry Condell, Shakespeare's first publishers, worshipped. A memorial, topped by a bronze bust of the Bard, reminds us of the debt we owe these 'heroes of the First Folio'. This stands as the centerpiece of a raised paved seating area, with drought tolerant planting, in what was once the churchyard. A pretty knot garden completes the trio of gardens.

St Lawrence Jewry

An awkward corner site outside the Corporation of London's official church – a Wren creation extensively rebuilt following war damage. It has been ingeniously transformed into a water garden. The pond is planted with water lilies, irises and bulrushes and is home to a large resident carp. Blocks of evergreen hedging tactfully indicate the garden's street boundary.

St Mary Aldermanbury

Girdlers' Hall Space

Although the Girdler's Company is in possession of an award winning walled private garden behind their classically styled livery hall, it's the recently revamped open space in front of it that will perhaps be more appreciated by workers in search of somewhere to enjoy their lunchtime sandwich. Owned by the Corporation of London, the site, at the intersection of Basinghall Avenue and Coleman Street, is a lovely example of their 'green corners' policy with its crisp arrangement of parallel lines of box hedging, interplanted with soft, billowy grasses, ferns and acanthus, multi-stemmed trees, and possibly the lushest stretch of lawn in EC2. Seating for weary City folk takes the form of granite blocks or more forgiving wooden benches and chairs. From here the doll's house like proportions of the Girdlers' Hall can be admired, against the backdrop of City Tower, which looms in the distance.

C Clifton Nurseries

Whether you're commissioning a bespoke garden for your house or just after a pot of basil for your kitchen windowsill, Clifton Nurseries have got all the angles covered.

Hidden behind the blandly elegant white stucco houses of Little Venice, the nursery is a haven for horticultural shoppers, offering a comprehensive portfolio of services – from irrigation systems to 'Assisted DIY' garden maintenance, flower arrangements and even a plant storage facility (for when you've got the builders in). And it's no johnny-come-lately either, tracing its origins as a 'nursery ground' as far back at 1851; its enterprising owner in the late 1800s did a roaring trade hiring plants out to London's hotels, theatres and, later, film studios. However by the late 1970s Clifton was facing an uncertain future until Lord Jacob Rothschild bought the nursery in 1979. Since then the nurseries' historic

premises have been graced by an award winning shop building (designed by Jeremy Dixon) and a new Palm House, built in the spirit of a predecessor on the site. In recent years the nursery's horticultural expertise has also been awarded 5 Gold Medals from Chelsea Flower Show (see p.50).

For all the impressive architecture, this is still a great place to buy plants – the Palm House is home to an eclectic stock of indoor plants including fragrant gardenia, jungly palms and ferns, cacti and carnivorous plants as well as some flamboyant imitation blooms. Outside, the main plant display area caters for city gardeners with grasses and evergreens, topiary, seasonal herbaceous plants, bulbs and herbs. If they don't have what you're looking for, the nursery can order it and also offer advice on the right plant for the right place. Some of the stock is grown at Clifton's sister site, the nursery

garden at Waddesdon Manor in Buckinghamshire, while as much as possible of the remainder is sourced from London and the South-East – cutting down on 'plant miles' and ensuring that plants are acclimatised. In summer the glass topped arcade that extends out from the palm house shelters a colourful mass of bedding plants, including deluxe hanging baskets, and is also home to a luxuriant grape vine, whose edible fruits dangle temptingly at harvest time. For those in search of containers, there's a comprehensive selection of pots from sturdy frost-proof salt-glazed ceramics to classic wooden Versailles planters and trendy zinc tubs. Lifestyle needs are further addressed in the shop, which deals with the furnishings, cushions and candles side of gardening, as well as more gritty gardeners' fare like composts, tomato feed, tools and seeds. An on-site garden design studio and a café with outside seating completes the set up.

Clifton Nurseries
5A Clifton Villas, Little Venice, W9 2PH
www.clifton.co.uk   T: 020 7289 6851
Open: Mon-Sat 9.00-18.00 (Apr-Oct),
Mon-Sat 8.30 to 17.30 (Nov-Mar),
every Sun (except Easter) 11.00-17.00

Cloistered away next to the historic Priory Church of St John, this fragrant garden is part of the Museum of the Order of St John, which tells the 900 year-old story of the Knights of St John. As members of an Order of the church, the Knights also had medical and military roles, setting up hospitals in the Holy Land and Europe, while fighting in defence of Christendom. Today, the modern Order of St John is best known for establishing the St John Ambulance.

The garden's planting scheme was devised by London-based designer Alison Wear, to fit in around the existing hard-landscaping, and is packed with references to the Order's long peregrination around Europe, with silver-leaved Mediterranean sun-seekers like *Phlomis fruticosa* (Jerusalem sage) and medicinal herbs such as *Hypericum calycinum* (St John's Wort), *Lychnis chalcedonica* (Maltese or Jerusalem cross), and a white rose, *Rosa* 'St John'. Aromatic herbs such as wormwood, thyme, oregano, fennel and lavender further recall the Knights' medical endeavours, while creating a soothingly aromatic environment for the visitor.

Working within the constraints of the layout, Alison designed for colour and texture rather than harmony or sophistication, using citrus and olive trees in strategically placed tubs to break up the formal setting. Winter interest is provided by aromatic evergreens such as *Daphne odora*, bay and box. When it came to planting in April 2011, Alison found that the soil was 'nothing but dust', so an 'enormous amount' of compost and manure was applied to the narrow beds. The strategy is working and with museum staff undertaking to water the fledgling plants in the absence of an irrigation system, the garden already appears remarkably well-established.

Museum of the Order of St John
St John's Gate, St John's Lane, EC1M
www.museumstjohn.org.uk   T: 020 7324 4005
Admission free (small donation suggested for tours)

Alison Wear Garden Design
www.alisonwear.com

Columbia Road Market is a London institution – a photogenic relic of the old East End that has somehow survived into the 21st century. A true hardy perennial, this flower and plant market is open every Sunday of the year (unless Christmas Day falls on a Sunday), and is a favourite haunt of budget conscious London gardeners. Over the past few years this unique market has become popular with tourists too, and teaming crowds can at times make this shop-lined Victorian street difficult to navigate, particularly if you've got an armful of plants to deliver safely home.

The market runs from 8am until around 3pm but is at its busiest between about 10.30am and 1pm. This presents shoppers with a dilemma: early birds get a clear run and the pick of the stock, latecomers have less choice and elbow room but more bargains, as prices plummet as the day draws to a close. This is a great place to kit your garden out on the cheap as some of the impressively well-stocked gardens in the immediate vicinity suggest – there's a particularly verdant example on the corner of Chambord Street. With about 50 stalls there's a surprisingly adventurous range of plant life on offer – from citrus trees to colourful seasonal bedding to elegant orchids and trusty herbaceous perennials. If your cutting garden is yet to come on stream, there are plenty of specialist cut flower stalls too, selling keenly priced, great quality blooms and foliage for spectacular arrangements. An eclectic range of independent shops complements the market stalls – a choice which embraces cafés, milliners, contemporary furniture, art galleries, garden equipment and vintage bric-a-brac.

Stall holders are a friendly lot and, when not belting out their sales patter are happy to dispense advice and growing tips. Most of the traders hail from Essex where many have their own nurseries, like David Williams of Oak Royal Nurseries in Cranham. He has been doing Columbia Road since 1972 and deals in unusual shrubs, perennials and alpines – his stock includes ornamental grasses such as *Pennisetum orientale*, perennials like

Heuchera 'Blackberry Jam', and *Leptospermum*, (from New Zealand where it is more commonly known as manuka). His regular customers include gardening clubs who visit the market by the coach load. Market representative George Gladwell has a nursery at Langdon Hills, Basildon – and is the go-to man for bulbs or perennials or to arrange a spot of filming (the market is a popular location). Another grower is Lyndon Osborn, whose nursery is in High Barnet. Lyndon specialises in what he calls 'London plants' – mainly shade loving or tolerant plants which can cope with London's built-up landscape which he sees as a giant woodland. Being grown so close

to the city his plants have a low carbon footprint and are acclimatised to London's growing conditions; antipodean tree ferns are the showy stars on his stall but you can also spot the likes of *Aeoniums*, *Salvias*, *Plectranthus* (hardy and tender varieties) and *Artemisia*. Stall holder Anthony Burridge (one of many Burridge's on the market) takes a different approach, buying 'leftovers' from Dutch wholesalers to sell them at a discount on the market. His stock changes every week and is a great place to look for plant bargains.

To make the most of the market come prepared with cash, suitable bags or a trolley and a good idea of what you want to buy – otherwise you will get seriously led astray with impulse buys. There are lots of deals for buying in bulk and things get even cheaper as the day goes on. It's a great idea to go with a friend and combine your buying power.

Columbia Road Market, E2 7RG
www.columbiaroad.info
Open: Sundays 8.00-15.00

A few things to look out for when buying plants (whether you are buying them at a market or not):

- Plants that look healthy probably are – choose plants that have strong, even growth and a nice shape; check for signs of pests or disease such as discoloured leaves, holes in leaves or ragged edges.

- Check for healthy roots that fill the pot (if roots are growing out through the bottom the plant is pot bound and should be avoided). Carefully upend pot and pull away from plant – while inspecting roots also look for signs of unwanted insect life.

- Plants should be clearly labelled; varieties that have been awarded the RHS Award of Garden Merit (AGM) are particularly good buys as they have been rigorously tested for hardiness, pest and disease resistance.

- Don't be afraid to buy plants in bloom – you can see exactly what you're getting and whether or not it's going to work in your garden.

- When buying bulbs – check that bulbs are firm with no signs of pests or disease.

C Container Gardening

Window boxes, balconies and roof gardens… where would the garden-less Londoner be without containers? Even those lucky enough to have a garden of their own often choose to supplement their borders with a strategically placed container or two, for an extra kick of seasonal colour, to fill in a bald patch, or simply because they have a beautiful plant pot to show off.

And whether they be a traditional hand-thrown terracotta long-tom or a rusty old dustbin, containers are ideal for gardeners who like to change their planting schemes on a whim or who enjoy mixing it up with plant combinations

that wouldn't be possible in nature. Container gardening is tailor-made too for London's serial renters – moving your garden is a cinch if your plants are housed in portable pots.

Of course, there is a price for all this versatility; like having a demanding pet, container gardening requires commitment. Your plants will be totally dependent on you to water and feed them, a daily chore (twice daily in hot weather) that can make holidays and weekends away fraught with anxiety. Capillary matting and automatic irrigation systems are one solution, reciprocal watering arrangements with like-minded neighbours another.

C Coriander Club

For the ladies of the Coriander Club there's no taste like home and here in the raised beds and polytunnels of Spitalfields City Farm is where they can find it, growing the Bangladeshi vegetables and herbs that are hard to source in the UK.

In Bangladesh it is traditional for women to grow their own food but this is not so easy in Tower Hamlets, one third of whose population is Bangladeshi. Coriander Club founder Lutfun

Hussain set up the women-only group in 2000 as a place where Bangladeshi and other women could get together to socialize and exercise whilst gardening: 'It's good to share and it's really nice to work with others in the garden.'

Lutfun brings with her years of expertise in raising Bangladeshi crops such as kodu, snake gourd, Indian mustard, chillies and even rice in Britain's cool climate. From a farming background, she has been gardening in London since her arrival in 1969 and by trial and error has worked out what succeeds in this country. Crops like aramanth, aubergines, chillies and enormous kodu gourds are cosseted in the cosy confines of the polytunnels while coriander, climbing beans and mooli (a kind of giant radish) are tough enough to grow outside. Other outdoor crops include veg plot stalwarts like potatoes, carrots, onions, tomatoes and pumpkins (which race like unruly children through the raised beds and well beyond). Produce is shared amongst members, but word-of-mouth ensures any surplus finds ready buyers. A spirit of generosity pervades the garden and Lutfun says, 'Sometimes people come to find food for a sick relative and I always try to save some for these people. It is always a comfort to taste food from home when you are not well.'

Sustainability is central to Lutfun's approach and she runs the garden organically, making full use of the farm's manure, and saving seeds for sowing the following year. Cheerful blooms such as tagetes, calendula, sunflowers and dahlias appear in profusion around the site, keeping the insect population happy. Such is the garden's productivity that it is a regular winner at the annual gathering of community gardeners at Capel Manor in September (one of Lutfun's favourite gardening events along with the Chelsea Flower Show). The farm's proximity to the City makes it popular with corporate volunteers, who get stuck in helping Lutfun with gardening tasks or undertake bigger team challenges like fencing.

Pick and cook sessions are held twice monthly and Lutfun often prepares food on site to show visitors more about her native cuisine. The Coriander Club has also produced a cookbook with recipes showcasing the Bangladeshi ingredients it grows at the farm.

Spitalfields City Farm, Buxton Street, E1 5AR
www.spitalfieldscityfarm.org   T: 020 7247 8762

Lutfun Hussain

Culpeper Community Garden

From derelict bombsite to multi-award winning garden, the Culpeper has come a long way since the early 80s when the site began to be developed as a public garden.

Transformed by the community for the community, this triangular plot of land now brims with plants and buzzes with wildlife, a verdant oasis in the depths of urban Islington. The layout is a model of clever planning, serpentine paths weave around the garden offering a choice of routes, each one as beguiling as the next, and making the space feel bigger than it is. On your journey you may pass a rockery, a picnic lawn, a herb garden, a frog-filled pond, as well as the 40 or so mini allotment style plots tended by community groups, children, disabled gardeners and local people who don't have a garden of their own. In spring snowdrops and bluebells usher in the new season while in June the pergola is festooned with roses and the garden is saturated with the colourful blooms of annuals and herbaceous perennials. Insects and birds love it here, the diversity of plants, from vegetables and herbs to native trees and shrubs provide a great range of habitats. Woodpeckers, finches – green and gold – and dragonflies are just some of creatures who have made this their home. The garden has an organic and sustainable approach and in 2008 a new community centre was completed. The centre fully embodies the garden's philosophy with eco-features such as green roof, and a water collection system to keep the pond topped up with rainwater.

People as well as plants flourish in this atmospheric garden – on any given day you may find groups of friends or families just chilling on the picnic lawn, children hunting for ladybirds or pond dipping, gardeners tending their plots or enjoying a cuppa and a chat at the tea hut. Events such as musical performances, gardening workshops, talks and

plants sales make the Culpeper a social hub too, and the community ethos is still strong with an annual pensioners strawberry tea and projects to cater for community groups, schools and disadvantaged groups such as asylum seekers.

Culpeper Community Garden
1 Cloudesley Road, N1
www.culpeper.org.uk
T: 020 7833 3951

D Dye Garden at Vauxhall City Farm

With its own on-site manure supply, there's no excuse for poor soil fertility in this garden. Compared to its country cousins, Vauxhall City Farm is tiny but its 1.5 acres are home to some 80 animals, including cows, horses, pigs, poultry and rare breed sheep, all producing the black gold so valued by gardeners.

Walking through the authentically aromatic farmyard, the visitor comes to the Community Garden. The first area is a Dye Garden, planted with all manner of colour-producing plants such as achillea (bronze/moss green), weld (bright yellow) and hollyhocks (grey-blue). The garden evolved from being a 'dye allotment' and was set up about 10 years ago by Diane Sullock. A millennium award paid for the garden's dramatic centrepiece, a raised spiral bed, while Diane grew many of the dye plants from seeds.

Today the plot is cultivated by the Spinners who have a workshop on the site. They are a group of about a dozen textile artists and craftsmen with Penny Walsh the lead designer. It's a model of sustainable enterprise: the Spinners make dyes from the plants to colour the wool produced by the farm's sheep and alpacas, spin the fibres into yarn, which in turn is woven into textiles. On Saturdays the Spinners run educational courses in dying, spinning and simple weaving and participants on 'dye days' help harvest the plants. Ironically, many dye plants, particularly the British natives, are not that colourful to look at and it is the roots of plants like the madder plant that produce the colour. However, the garden is far from monochrome with calendulas and, later in the season, dahlias providing a splash of cheery colour as well as being useful dye plants in their own right.

The second area of the garden is laid out with raised beds and is used as a therapeutic garden by the SLaM Horticultural Project, whose participants (from the South London & Maudsley NHS Foundation Trust) grow plants and vegetables as part of the healing process and as an aid to mental wellbeing. A small cluster of allotments at the far end of the plots gives growing space for local people.

Offering the sights, sounds and smells of the country in an ultra-urban setting, the farm attracts all sorts of visitors and users. It's a hive of activity, with riding lessons for disadvantaged children and the disabled, an active youth volunteer programme and popular 'Tour Talks' for schools groups. And just because you work in an office you needn't miss out on the fun – the farm's popular 'corporate challenges' gives the suited and booted the chance to get involved with team-building projects. The battered polytunnel in the garden being earmarked for just such a corporate makeover.

Vauxhall City Farm
Tyers Street, SE11
www.vauxhallcityfarm.org
T: 020 7582 4204
Open: Wed-Sun 10.30-16.00

Eltham Palace

Gardens don't come much more glamorous than the one which wraps itself around the heady architectural cocktail that is Eltham Palace.

Surprisingly rural in feel, given their SE9 location, the gardens gently complement the exotic union of the Great Hall built by Edward IV in the 15th century and the Art Deco mansion created for millionaire couple Stephen and Virginia Courtauld by architects Seely and Paget in the early 1930s. While there's more than a hint of Hollywood about Eltham's grande-luxe interior (a vision of sleek wood veneers, endless bathrooms and sweeping staircases) the garden is of the old-fashioned English Arts and Crafts variety, albeit one with its own moat and archaeological remains.

Despite the expense and care they lavished on Eltham, the Courtaulds only lived here for 8 years, moving out in 1944, so they never saw the gardens they planned come to maturity. English Heritage assumed responsibility for Eltham in 1995 and since then the gardens and house have been nurtured back to their 1930s glory. The garden retains a checklist of period features, including the obligatory herbaceous border and *ne plus ultra* of inter-war horticulture – a rock garden. However, while the Courtauld's employed a dozen or more gardeners, Eltham's 19 acres today are kept in trim by just 3 garden staff, with help from volunteers and outside contractors.

In high summer the 80 metre long herbaceous border, which unfolds along the foot of the south moat wall, puts on a high spirited display with puddles of soft purple-blue nepeta and acid yellow ladies' mantle spilling out on the gravel path, with spires of electric blue delphiniums nodding in the background, interspersed with sunny accents of achillea, golden rod and day lilies. White lupins and asters provide cooler tones, fiery notes come courtesy of geum and red crocosmia. The border was redesigned in 2000 by Isabelle van Groeningen and the artistry of the scheme can be savoured either at ground level or from on high – the wooden

bridge that spans the dry southern stretch of moat supplies a handy viewing platform. The ancient stone and brick walls of the moat soak up the summer heat, creating a toasty microclimate enjoyed by legions of butterflies but which makes weeding the back of the border hot work on sunny days.

Following the now dry course of the western moat, the sunken rose garden is another survivor of the Courtauld era. Planted with monoculture beds of hybrid musk and early hybrid tea roses and a surrounding lavender hedge, the rose garden is at its best in the summer. The two 'garden rooms' which follow on from it come into their own in the spring, when they are filled with the scent of *Daphne bholua*, with further colour provided by clusters of cream, dusky mauve and deep purple hellebores. Elsewhere in the garden scillas, daffodils, snowdrops, primroses, and wood anemones light up spare spring terrain.

Other classic 30's features include an island in the moat planted with a solitary weeping willow and, on the far bank of the Eastern moat, a precipitous rock garden. Created out of limestone, the rock garden still features some of its original trees but the heavy clay soil is not ideal and so this area has been predominantly replanted with shrubs. A cascade of water tumbles down the rock face into the moat, but for all its wild and rugged looks, the rock garden is difficult gardening terrain and with ever eager weeds, is more labour intensive than the herbaceous border. The stone loggia at the rear of the house offers an elevated vantage point over this part of the garden and is decorated with relief carved roundels celebrating the enthusiasms of its wealthy creators – Ginie's for horticulture and Stephen's interest in mountaineering (although he also was a keen horticulturalist, with a passion for orchids). The 19th-century Ionic columns which support the wisteria clad pergola here are a piece of suitably up-market architectural salvage, having been rescued from the Bank of England when it was redeveloped in the 1930s.

Visitors partaking of the light refreshments served in the excellent tea rooms (housed in Eltham's service wing) enjoy a ringside view of the 'triangular garden' designed by John Watkins. This garden room is divided up into brick paved lattice patterned compartments, and deploys a restful palette of soft silvers and golds, featuring sage, thyme, and red hot pokers. On a hot summer's day, with the windows open, birdsong from the garden competes with the tearooms' sound track of popular hits from the 30s and 40s.

The garden is managed as organically as possible, with the occasional spritz of glysophate on paths to keep weeds at bay. In spring a generous mulch of leaf mould or well-rotted manure is applied around the garden, with several tons of mulch going on the herbaceous border alone. As in the Courtauld's day, the far moat bank and parkland grasslands are managed traditionally, being left to flower and set seed before being cut for hay. In the summer this area is loud with insects and the garden as a whole is rich with wildlife – from the carp that silently patrol the moat to the dragonflies that skim across its surface, to woodpeckers, sparrowhawks and green parakeets that compete for airspace.

Designed as a place for entertaining (even in its Tudor incarnation the palace played host to foreign dignitaries and jousting tournaments), Eltham Palace still radiates an air of moneyed leisure. The Courtauld's home movies show how much they and their friends enjoyed Eltham's gardens, the outdoor antics usually being accompanied by a menagerie of assorted dogs, ducks, geese, goats and Stephen and Virginia's pet lemur, Mah-Jongg. Dogs (and presumably lemurs) are no longer welcome but visitors can still enjoy a picnic in Eltham's grounds. There is no better place in which to switch off from modern life and recapture those lost days of a pre-war English summer.

Eltham Palace
Court Yard, Eltham, Greenwich, SE9 5QE
www.english-heritage.org.uk
T: 020 8294 2548
Open: Sun-Wed 10.00-17.00 (Apr-Oct), 10.00-16.00
(Nov-March), closed January

F Fenton House

Tucked away in leafy, affluent Hampstead, Fenton House Garden is one of London's 'paradise' gardens. Like the original '*pairi. daêza*' of the ancient Middle East, the garden is walled and is home to an orchard, beehives, herb garden, kitchen garden as well as a flower garden and at least five wells.

Dating from the late 17[th]century, the time-mellowed red brick walls were built at the same time as the comfortable four-square merchant's house itself and the layout of the garden they enclose has changed little over three centuries.

The garden is broadly divided into two, the Flower Garden and the Kitchen Garden, with the former being planted to provide year-round interest with different areas 'performing' according to season. At the far end of the Flower garden, the North terrace is an Autumn border but with spring interest courtesy of bluebells and yellow tulips to kick-start the year. A dedicated Spring Border runs west alongside the neatly striped main lawn and is planted with cheery *Anemone blanda*, *Narcissi*, *Pulsatilla vulgaris* and *Genista hispada*. April and May are the time to enjoy this border, although later in the year the heady scent of *Philadelphus* makes this a place to linger. For summer fragrance the sunken Rose Garden is filled with heavily perfumed old-fashioned roses and lavender.

For many, late summer is the best time to visit this immaculately tended garden. In the Flower Garden, the inner edge of East Terrace brims with clouds of catmint, punctuated with planters overflowing with the vivid blue blooms of *Agapanthus* 'Navy Blue'. Enclosed by lofty yew hedges, the Cross Borders are also a haven for late flowering favourites such as silvery leafed *Perovskia atriplicifolia* 'Blue Spire' and *Artemisia* 'Powis Castle' as well as architectural plants like *Stipa gigantea* and *Eryngium*. Down in

the Kitchen Garden the apple trees are laden with fruit and even the vegetable beds are surrounded by espaliered fruit trees. Amazingly, this modestly sized orchard contains thirty different varieties of apples from historic types like the Devon Quarrendon (introduced 1676) to newfangled varieties like Discovery (1949). Harvested fruits are sold at the entrance porch to the house and there is also a small selection of plants for sale near the Glasshouse, charmingly operating on an honesty box system.

Fenton House
Hampstead Grove, Hampstead, NW3 6SP
www.nationaltrust.org.uk
T: 01494 755563 (Info line)
T: 020 7435 3471

The orchard, Fenton House

F Food from the Sky

Eight metres above street level, Food from the Sky is pioneering a rooftop revolution. Its collection of plastic recycling bins, wormeries, composters and old bathtubs might look ramshackle but they are the heart of a unique food growing and educational project.

Working in partnership with Andrew Thornton, the owner of Budgens supermarket in Crouch End, Azul-Valerie Thome has created a high-rise, perma-culture allotment growing organic food that is sold in the supermarket below. Harvesting takes place every Friday and invariably sells out by Sunday.

A self-styled 'seeder of change', Azul was inspired by a simple observation: that London's shortage of productive land could be addressed by using its plentiful supply of flat roofs. Evidently not your average supermarket boss, Andrew Thornton agreed and, having had the roof of his Crouch End supermarket surveyed for strength, Food from the Sky was born. Run as a community garden, with volunteer helpers, the project was set up as a Capital Growth project, with the support of Haringey Council, who donated three hundred recycling boxes to use as growing containers and 10 tonnes of compost. Everything was craned into place in May 2010 and the first produce went on sale in the supermarket in July.

The garden follows biodynamic growing rhythms and is a model of sustainability. Waste from the garden and from the supermarket is composted on site to create a growing medium, polystyrene blocks are used for drainage, seeds are saved or acquired through community seed swaps, and volunteers and visiting school parties learn about urban growing techniques while tending the plot. Food from the Sky has partnered with Heritage Seed Library to grow endangered heirloom varieties to sell 'downstairs'. In 2011 these varieties included Yellow Scotland and Grosse Lisse tomatoes, purple Russian kale and purple carrots.

Azul-Valerie Thome

As it turns out, food grows well 'in the sky' but rooftop horticulture offers some particular challenges with strong winds and the need for lots of watering. Reliance on mains water is one of the garden's weaknesses Azul acknowledges, but she is working on it. Pigeons and cats are the main pests up here and chicken wire and old CDs are used to protect vulnerable young plants against their unwanted attentions. Some crops have been more successful than others – Swiss chard grew well but was a disaster commercially as it wilted too quickly once picked. Leaf crops such as rocket, lettuce and kale, as well as herbs such as borage, and edible flowers like calendula have proved more reliable and sell well too. Thanks to the micro-climate generated cause by the supermarket's refrigeration system, the garden can still yield rocket every in mid winter.

Although rooted in the local, Azul's re-imagining of the relationship between community, supermarket and food growers is far from parochial and Food from the Sky has attracted interest from both home and abroad. To this end, Azul and her team have prepared a template, using their experience of setting up Food from the Sky, to help others who want to gather their own high rise harvest.

Thornton's Budgens, 21-23 The Broadway, N8 8DU
www.foodfromthesky.org.uk

F Front Gardens

Naomi Schillinger

Do Londoners love their cars more than their front gardens? In some boroughs it appears that they do – according to an influential report carried out by Ealing's Local Agenda 21, nearly a quarter of the borough's 74,300 front gardens are completely hard surfaced with no vegetation at all. And the problem is exacerbated by a 'domino effect' whereby the more front gardens are converted into parking spaces the less on-street parking is available, leading to more gardens being paved over. The trend looks set to continue, despite the 2008 planning regulation requiring planning permission for impermeable surfacing of more than 5 square metres.

However, with a bit of thoughtful design and the use of impermeable materials such as gravel, reinforced lawns and carefully chosen plants, it is perfectly possible for cars and front-gardens to cohabit. The 2011 RHS publication *Gardening Matters, Urban Series: Front Gardens* has some great ideas for car friendly gardens. Ealing Front Gardens Project hope to reinstate 3 front gardens in 2012, working with home-owners who want to restore their hard-surfaced gardens back to something softer.

They may be small but London's estimated 1.8 million front gardens cover some 9,400 hectares and have a big contribution to make to the capital's environmental and aesthetic well-being, providing important habitat for urban wildlife and a valuable focus for neighbourly interaction. Conversely, impermeable surfaces bring with them the increased risk of flooding, the creation of localized heat islands (which intensify the effects of heat waves), and contribute to a decline in biodiversity. Perhaps most importantly, paved gardens are just plain ugly.

In Islington one community gardening scheme has harnessed the positive potential of front gardens. The Blackstock Triangle Gardens Project was started in 2009 by neighbours Naomi Schillinger and Nicolette Jones and initially focused on treepits in the local roads. The following year, thanks to Capital Growth funding, they added a food growing dimension, with grow bags and free seeds being issued to 50 participants enabling them to raise sweetcorn, squash and beans in their front gardens. In 2011 the number of participants doubled to 100 and in an exciting development, funding was found for 10 front gardens to have their concrete removed and be reinstated as productive spaces. The project has also boosted community spirit with people getting to know their neighbours for the first time through their gardens, and friendships cemented over tea and cakes at popular 'Cake Sunday' events.

www.outofmyshed.co.uk/btg/
www.ealingfrontgardens.org.uk

Garden greenspace in the capital's gardens has been lost at a rate of two and a half Hyde Parks per year driven by recent trends in garden design

Caroline Davison

Maureen and David Herbert

Annie Monaghan

F Frugal Gardening Tips

Once the gardening bug has bitten it can be a surprise to discover how much your new addiction can cost – garden infrastructure, tools, plants and seeds can all be expensive to acquire and naturally there are no end of specialist companies eager to part you from your cash. Horticulture may be big business nowadays but there are plenty of ways of gardening on the cheap – and in fact, as allotment plots all over the land testify, most gardeners (and their gardens) thrive on the ingenuity required by a make-do-and-mend approach. Here are a few tips to get you started:

Collect seed from your plants

- Grow plants from seed – it may take longer but it's far cheaper and more satisfying and you can choose exactly the variety you want (see appendix for suggested seed companies and for inspiration read *A Garden from a Hundred Packets of Seed* by James Fenton, Viking 2001.

- Seed exchange events are a great place to pick up seeds for free or a small donation. If you're buying seeds, the chances are you won't use all of them in a season so get together with gardening friends to swap seeds – that way you'll get more varieties and perhaps try out ones you wouldn't normally grow.

- Collect seed from your plants to use the following season (see left); surplus seeds can be swapped with friends or via a seed exchange forum like www.gardenswapshop.org.uk.

- Plant stands at your local horticultural society or gardening club can often be a great place to pick up cheap and unusual plants (though don't be shy about checking the root ball for unwanted weeds or pests).

- Ditto car boot sales, jumble sales, church fêtes.

- Take cuttings – don't be afraid to ask friends with established gardens. Propagating from plants is straightforward and can be quicker than growing from seed. Roses, lavender, penstemon, pelargoniums are all dead easy to propagate and with the advantage that because you are essential making a clone of the parent plant you know exactly what variety you are getting (not always the case with seeds).

- Once they get going, plants are amazingly good at reproducing – cottage garden favourites like poppies, pot marigold, nasturtiums, columbines are prodigious self-seeders. Dig up the unwanted seedlings and plant elsewhere or swap or sell them.

- Clump forming herbaceous perennials like sedum, geraniums, asters, daisies, grasses and oriental poppies can be divided in spring (and sometimes autumn) to make more plants to fill your garden or to swap or sell.

- Terracotta pots are beautiful and their porosity makes them perfect for raising plants but they can be pricey. Be imaginative about containers – as long as there are drainage holes in the bottom anything from an old olive oil can to a wellington boot can become a 'plant pot'. Rubber tyres make good raised beds for the allotment or veg patch.

An old bath can make a great container

- Yes, it is perfectly possibly to germinate seeds on your window sills but you may find that your gardening ambition will quickly outgrow the available space inside your own dwelling. Your dreams will be haunted by visions of gleaming greenhouses, packed with pristine produce and radiant blooms. No need to splash out on a new one though – scour your local small ads or Freecycle for unwanted greenhouses in search of a new home (I got my little lean-to greenhouse from a neighbour who had bought a larger one). Polytunnels are a cheaper alternative to greenhouses and the web is awash with instructions on how to make your own if you want to save even more money.

Wheelbarrow – a movable container!

- Harvest your own water. It may cost a little to install a water butt or two but it's better for the environment and your plants to recycle rainwater for garden use. If you are on a water meter, you may even save some money.

- Make your own compost – it's an eco-friendly way of adding goodness to your garden soil and getting rid of kitchen waste (but not cooked food or meat). If you don't have a garden, a wormery on your balcony or in your backyard will produce small quantities of top quality compost that can be used potting purposes. Mark Ridsdill Smith makes great use of his wormery (see p.220).

Make your own compost

G The Garden Museum

A redundant church on a congested intersection in Lambeth, is a surprising venue for this museum celebrating the joys of gardening, past and present. In some ways however the location is perfectly fitting, for its churchyard cum garden contains the tomb of the Tradescants, 17th-century plant hunters and Royal gardeners. Their collection of curiosities and specimens became the basis of Britain's first university museum, the Ashmolean (whose eponymous founder, Elias Ashmole, is also buried here).

Developed into two distinct garden areas – a blowsy wild garden to the front and a beautifully recreated 17th-century knot garden to the rear – the churchyard remains a sanctuary from the relentless city beyond. The wild bit is a relatively new creation, first planted in 2007, and is a model of biodiversity, attracting not only city workers on their lunch-break but a plethora of insect and bird life. Nectar rich plants are the order of the day – an informal meadow style planting scheme features a riot of opium poppies, red and white valerian, harebells, cow parsley, knapweed and snakeshead fritillary. The garden is 'mown' by hand once a year in August or September, and the seed heads allowed to fall to the ground before being raked up a couple of weeks later.

The knot garden is a much more ordered affair and has been in place since 1981. Designed by the Dowager Marchioness of Salisbury, the knot is an intricate geometric design planted with historically authentic 17th-century plants. Within its formal box hedges grow damask and gallica roses, peonies and cotton lavender as well as cottage garden favourites like foxgloves, honesty and love-in-a-mist. Among the perennials can be found *Tradescantia virginiana*, named in honour of the Tradescants, while at the knot's centre a magnificent spiral holly topiary, the suitably regal *Ilex x altaclerensis* 'Golden King', holds court. The surrounding borders have been planted with similar attention to period authenticity, with a few exceptions including a banana tree,

which shows its appreciation of the garden's mild microclimate by overwintering and occasionally producing juvenile fruit. Although its walls and plants can't quite keep out the traffic noise, the knot garden is a nevertheless an enchanting place to while away some time with a book, a friend or a coffee.

Inside the problems of putting a modern museum inside a historic church have been partially solved by a new interior, made from pale wood, by architects Dow Jones. This has created a mezzanine floor where a compact selection of the permanent collection is displayed – an eclectic and entertaining mix of tools and gardenalia. People often liken gardening to warfare and the vintage tools on show are good evidence of this, with lethal implements ranging from heavy duty weeding and turfing kit used by professional gardeners, to elegant horticultural weaponry designed for the 'gentleman gardener'. Other exhibits include paintings and photographs, books and ephemera such as seed packets.

The ground floor hosts temporary exhibitions, whose themes reflect the museum's aim of capturing 'the garden zeitgeist' and which have included 'The Good Life' and a retrospective of dry gardening guru Beth Chatto. This level is also home to a shop well stocked with gardening goodies and an excellent vegetarian café. Despite the museum's recent redevelopment, the latter retains its rather rustic air and is a great place for a light lunch or home baked cake, or indeed both. The much sought after outdoor seating in the knot garden is reached via a 'potting shed' – a hub of seasonal advise and tasks guaranteed to send you scurrying back to your own garden, trowel in hand.

The Garden Museum
Lambeth Palace Road, SE1 7LB
020 7401 8865
Info@gardenmuseum.co.uk
www.gardenmuseum.co.uk
Daily 10.30-17.00, Saturday 10.30-16.00
Admission charge

Bligh tomb

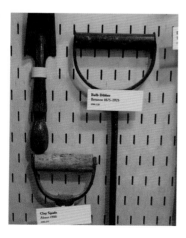

The Knot Garden

Geffrye Museum Garden

Best known as the museum of English home, the Geffrye has another, rather less well publicised, string to its bow. Its evocative collection of period rooms – housed in a gracious early 18th-century almshouse – is complemented by a suite of historic gardens and an abundantly stocked herb garden, tucked away behind the museum.

With outside space at a premium these historic gardens are necessarily compact but offer a succinct 'edited highlights' tour of the English urban back garden through the centuries. Developed in 1998, the garden rooms – like their interior counterparts – focus on middle-class taste and although not recreating any individual gardens, care has been taken to ensure planting choices and relationships are historically accurate. In a further symmetry, whilst the museum's furniture collection reflects this part of London's association with the furniture industry, the gardens and herb garden reference the market gardens and nurseries for which this area was also once renowned.

A 16th-century knot garden is the first in the sequence – its sinuous knots are described by grey leaved *Santolina chamaecyparissus* and wall germander (*Teucrium chamaedrys*), and its intricate design derived from Renaissance decorative arts. With our modern interest in growing vegetables, deep bed growing and herbs, the Late Elizabethan garden looks reassuringly familiar with its sturdy raised wooden beds, planted with useful plants – aromatic herbs for culinary, medicinal and cosmetic purposes and pretties such as peonies, cowslips and roses.

Showing off your prize specimens was the name of the game for mid to late Georgian gardeners – the town garden recreated here is simple but decorative, reflecting the garden's increasing role as an 'outside room'. Three circular box-edged beds are planted with a central box ball and a few choice seasonal specimens such as candytuft (*Iberis sempervirens*) and *Fritillaria imperialis* – unlike modern gardeners,

the Georgians were not dismayed by the sight of bare earth between their plants. An auricula theatre is another opportunity for the display of rare and valued plants – May is the ideal time to inspect these orderly blooms grandstanding in their specially constructed playhouse.

The Victorians however liked nothing more than densely planted carpet bedding – preferably using the brightest colours available. The mid-19th century garden evoked at the Geffrye has an annual bedding display which has recently included a 'pelargonium pyramid' – an early take on today's mania for 'vertical planting'. A small but perfectly formed glasshouse – the kind gardeners then and now would kill for – completes this picture of cosy domesticity. Containing African violets, pelargoniums and ferns, its contents reflect the Victorians' enthusiasms for tender and exotic plants.

Relaxed and cottagey are the key words for the Edwardian garden – a pastoral rejection of the formality of the preceding era. Visitors in May can inhale the intense perfume of the blowsy purple wisteria on the Lutyenseque brick pillared pergola, those in June can admire its companion, a climbing rose, in bloom (the latter a favoured nesting place for resident blue tits). The border here features the likes of Geranium x magnificum, Bergenia, Aquilegia, and a lovely Rose 'Irene Watts' and Peony 'Baroness Schroeder'.

Returning back through the enfilade of period garden rooms, one comes to the Herb Garden – the most established of the Geffrye gardens, having been planted in 1992. This walled space – once derelict land adjacent to the museum – is a traditionally arranged herb garden, centred around a specially commissioned bronze fountain by Kate Malone. Now beautifully mature, the garden contains over 170 different herbs with a variety of different applications from the medicinal to the cosmetic.

The Herb Garden

Auricula theatre

Nectar rich plants such as anise hyssop, golden rod and sage attract visiting bees and there is also a section devoted to dye plants such as rose madder and lady's bedstraw. With the 21st century's newfound enthusiasm for herbal medicine, the red warning labels flagging up poisonous herbs such as monkshood, are a useful warning to novice herbalists that nature's larder should be exploited with caution.

Overlooked by Hoxton station, the garden cannot claim to be the quietest in town but the new East London Line station has benefited the museum with visitor numbers increasing thanks to nosy travellers having their curiosity piqued as they look down on the Geffrye gardens from the elevated railway platforms. The diverse plant life and a chemical free regime, means that the Geffrye garden is a popular destination too for local wildlife – including butterflies, foxes and assorted bird species, from tiny darting wrens to starlings bathing themselves with joyful abandon in the herb garden fountain. Blackfly are less welcome visitors but numbers are managed using a spray solution of Ecover washing up liquid. The gardeners here (two full time, plus several volunteers) also have to cope with soil that is typically heavy London clay. An annual mulching of some 20 or so tons of farmyard manure, delivered in the depths of winter, helps ramp up the organic content.

The historic gardens are open 1 April-31 October but the museum's spacious front garden can be enjoyed year-round. It has recently been renovated to bring its appearance more in line with its days as an almshouse – and its lawns and mature trees are a green space much valued by locals and visitors.

The Geffrye Museum
136 Kingsland Road, E2 8EA
www.geffrye-museum.org.uk   T: 020 7739 9893
Gardens Open: 1 April-31 Oct during museum hours
Museum open: Tues-Sat 10.00-17.00, Sun & Bank Hols 12.00-17.00
Admission Free

The Edwardian Garden

Wilf and Gail Downing's exuberant front garden in Hackney is one of a trio on the same street that open for the National Garden Scheme. The Downings have lived here since the early 70s but the garden didn't get going until a few years later, when they were able to cut down the large privet hedge at the front. With the light flooding in, the garden began to take shape and has developed over the years with Wilf in charge of digging and hard landscaping and Gail taking care of the planting and design.

Having inherited unyielding London clay, Gail and Wilf opt for John Innes as their growing medium and source their plants from a local garden centre, as well as swapping plants with their garden-minded neighbours. The couple maximize their small space by going upwards, with colourful plants cascading from the window boxes on the first floor and by, guerrilla-style, extending outwards and 'pimping' their pavement with an eclectic selection of plant filled containers, including dustbins.

On a busy road, the garden attracts much admiration from passing pedestrians and drivers and in 2011 won the 'Pavement' category of the Conservation Foundation's Green Corners awards. These awards celebrate London's unsung gardening heroes who do their bit to make the capital a greener place with school green corners, edible green corners and sacred spaces among the categories awarded. Worthy winners, Wilf and Gail enjoy opening for the NGS, although as Wilf points out, 'It's a front garden – it's open to everybody!'

Alexandra Park Gardens, N22 7BG
www.ngs.org.uk
www.conservationfoundation.co.uk

"*I like digging – it gives me great satisfaction!*"

Wilf Downing

G Guerrilla Gardener

Since he first began blogging about his illicit gardening activities in 2004, Richard Reynolds has almost single-handedly turned the underground business of being a guerrilla gardener into a high-profile occupation.

Recently voted the 24th most influential gardener in Britain, Reynolds (aka @Richard_001) has taken the Duchess of Cornwall on a tour of guerrilla gardens in London, designed a GG themed installation in Selfridges, and had his book *On Guerrilla Gardening* translated into French, German and Korean.

Reynolds defines guerrilla gardening as gardening land without permission – this is usually public land but in some cases more adventurous guerilla gardeners have trespassed onto private land to wield their hoes. Reynolds undertook his first covert mission in the neglected flower beds outside Peronnet House, the residential block in Elephant & Castle where he lives. He recalls, 'I thought, right, I'm going to sort this out, I don't want to complain about it, I want to have the fun of doing it myself.'

With gardening in his DNA – both his mother and grandmother are avid gardeners – Reynolds was unfazed by the challenges of unauthorised urban gardening. Once embarked on cultivation of obviously neglected land, he found the powers-that-be were usually happy to turn a blind eye. Indeed, on occasion, they have even been known to take the credit for the hard, often nocturnal, work put in by Richard and his fellow guerrillas.

As more troops have rallied to 'fight the filth with forks and flowers', Richard's forthright approach to his obsessive hobby has evolved into something that might even be termed 'responsible guerrilla gardening'. Careful now not to overcommit himself too far from home, he ensures local guerrillas are in place to care for new gardens being created, since well-maintained plots are less likely to be a target for vandals and litter.

Frustrated by the 'professionalization' of gardening as seen on TV, Reynolds has harnessed the informality of social networking media to encourage

"My main aim is to provide some sort of inspiration for other people, for them to just go and do it in their area, as befits their motivations and their particular landscape."

"Cheap, colourful and low-maintenance stuff is what I'm after – the kind of things you wouldn't expect local authorities to plant".

would-be guerrillas to 'just get stuck in – learn from your mistakes and if something dies, try something else'. His snappy website has become the global hub of the guerrilla gardening movement from where Reynolds launched 'Pimp your Pavement', a campaign to liven up London's sidewalks through the power of plants.

Consistent aftercare aside, cheap, practical plant choices are essential to successful guerrilla campaigns, and Richard recommends easy, gently invasive annuals such as calendula, nigella and Californian poppies that provide lots of colour over a long season. Sunflowers are another GG favourite and the focus of International Sunflower Guerrilla Gardening Day, held every May Day (its autumn counterpart is International Tulip Day). Richard's own preferred guerrilla plant is fragrant, evergreen lavender and it features in his favourite stealth garden, the 'lavender field' near Lambeth North tube – 'it's the largest one I look after and the most spectacular. It's the best place to garden because of the conversations I have with passers-by. They are so happy with it, particularly when the lavender is in full bloom and covered in bumble bees. You can smell it before you see it!'

www.guerrillagardening.org
www.pimpyourpavement.com

This page & opposite: Lavender Fields, Lambeth North Tube Station, SE1

H   Hall Place and Gardens

Bexley's excellent local history museum is also a compelling destination for garden lovers. Hall Place itself is a historic house with a split personality – one half a flint and rubble Tudor hall, the other a smart red brick 17th-century mansion. The 65 hectares of award-winning gardens that surround it, also reflect this diversity.

Close to the house is a series of formal gardens – a knot garden, a white border, two lengthy herbaceous borders, and topiary lawn guarded by a procession of heraldic beasts sculpted in yew. This unusual menagerie was planted in 1953 to celebrate the Queen's Coronation – the animals depict royal genealogy, the Falcon representing the Plantagenets for example. The yews have been trimmed and tied three times a year since their planting and were in good shape to celebrate the Diamond Jubilee in 2012. These fearsome creatures overlook a well-stocked rose garden, whose glorious colours and delicious scents make this a must-see (and a must smell) attraction in June. Elsewhere, simple arrangements of lavender hedges, pleached trees, and stripy lawns strike a more modern note.

The river Cray is the watery dividing line between the manicured gardens and the stately unfolding of landscaped parkland beyond. Here can be found, amongst other things, a wildflower meadow, mature specimen trees, oodles of wildlife and a heather garden (at its best in early spring). As if this wasn't enough, the old walled gardens are laid out with a sequence of 'demonstration' gardens, a well-labelled kitchen garden and a small orchard. The palm house is modern and functional, but crammed with exotics with crops like peanuts, sweet potatoes, coffee, avocados and kumquats. On an educational note, there is a planted timeline showing the sequence of botanical introductions to the Western world and – harking back to Hall Place's origins – a 'really useful' Tudor herb garden.

Bourne Road, Bexley, DA5 1PQ
www.hallplace.org.uk   T: 01322 526574
Historic House, visitor centre, glasshouse & café open daily 10.00-17.00
Gardens & parkland: Open daily 9.00-dusk
Admission free to gardens, visitor centre & Café
Wheelchair access

Above: Topiary lawn and the Queen's heraldic beasts
Opposite: Knot garden

H Ham House

Back in the day – the 17th century to be precise – this imposing Thameside mansion was a hotbed of political intrigue.

During the Commonwealth, the beautiful and wily Duchess of Lauderdale played a daring game, secretly working for the Royalist cause whilst openly pursuing a friendship with Oliver Cromwell. With Charles II restored to the throne the house became an important hub of the Restoration court, its fine interiors and stately gardens a reflection of the family's status at the heart of the royal court. Today Ham House is run by the National Trust, which began restoring the gardens to their 17th-century layout in 1975, using the original 1671 plan as a basis for their reconstruction.

Approaching from the Thames, the visitor is greeted by a statue of Old Father Thames, stationed outside the Jacobean front of the house like a grizzled old family retainer. Neatly clipped bay drums and yew pyramids patrol the perimeter of the entrance front garden, overseen by stern looking busts set in the surrounding wall. The Coade stone pineapples on the front fence sound a more welcoming note, the exotic fruit being a symbol of hospitality and a signal of the Lauderdale family's love of entertaining.

Moving clockwise around the grounds the Cherry Garden is the next space one encounters. Named for the morello cherry trees which once grew here, it's a dignified essay in topiary with diamond shaped box hedged compartments, punctuated with neat hand-clipped cones and soft mounds of grey leaved lavender. A marble statue of Bacchus hovers centre stage, where the gravel paths intersect. Visitors arriving on a hot summer's day will appreciate the shady sanctuary of the twin pleached hornbeam tunnels running along either side of the garden.

The south terrace – which fronts the Carolean side of the house – ushers in a change of mood and scale.

This broad gravel path is edged on the house side by a border planted in 17th-century style and filled with appropriate plants: lychnis (rose campion), echinops, echinacea, valerian, and flowering shrubs like hibiscus interspersed with slender cones of yew. To the left of the house is a weathered brick wall, to the right, an evergreen hedge – both perfect foils to the rosy pink accents of the flowers in the herbaceous border. A collection of large scale terracotta pots ramps up the drama of the terrace, below which lies the expanse of the 'plats' – a quintessentially 17th-century garden feature consisting of eight immaculate squares of lawn, intersected by dazzlingly pale gravel paths. Beyond the plats, lies another period garden, the 'wilderness'. This slightly misleading term (many of us will wish our wildernesses looked this tidy) actually denotes a formal wooded area divided up by a Union Jack type arrangement of radiating grassy paths, bordered by hornbeam hedges, behind which are concealed compartments containing four circular gazebos.

To the west of the house lies the Orangery Kitchen garden – a shadow of its 17th-century self with only four beds out of a possible 16 planted up (in its heyday the garden would have been twice as big, with a further 16 beds extending beyond the avenue of Quercus ilex). Vegetables, herbs and espaliered fruit are attractively grown here, on organic lines using companion planting and avoiding chemicals. The fresh produce is put to good use by the café, which is based in the elegant brick 17th-century Orangery. One of the oldest examples of its type in the country, in early summer the Orangery's facade is clothed in billowing clouds of purple wisteria, making the outside seating option particularly appealing.

Ham St, Ham, Richmond-upon-Thames, TW10 7RS
www.nationaltrust.org.uk/hamhouse
T: 020 8940 1950
House open: Sat-Wed 12.00-16.00 (March-Nov)
Garden open: Daily 11am-18.00

A Matter of Urgency, designer Jill M W Foxley

Hampton Court Flower Show

The extrovert younger sibling of the Chelsea Flower Show came of age in 2010, celebrating its 21st birthday with a bumper crop of show gardens, gigantic floral marquee and a major new 'Home Grown' exhibit.

Luxuriating in the spacious grounds of Hampton Court Palace the event has grown into the UK's biggest gardening show, covering a whopping 34 acres and pulling in annual crowds of over 160,000. The operation may be on a grand scale and the RHS standards as rigourous as ever but the vibe is relaxed – Hampton Court is noticeably less stuffy than Chelsea and has a greater emphasis on inclusivity, the environment, and growing your own. And – good news for plantaholics – unlike at Chelsea, plants are freely available for sale throughout the duration of the show, and there are even handy plant and product crèches where purchases can be parked for the day.

With over 600 hundred exhibitors vying for your attention, it can be difficult to know where to turn first; most visitors tend to spend around 5 hours at the show, so be strategic and pace yourself. The catalogue may seem an unnecessary extra expense on top of the ticket price but it's worth picking one up to really get a grip of the where, what and when of the show.

As at Chelsea, on arrival most visitors make a bee line for the Show Gardens; these meticulous installations will have taken three weeks to build, months to plan and are tended assiduously throughout the show so that visitors as well as the judges see them at their best. Once the judging has been completed and medals awarded the gardens are opened up to the public who can walk through them and admire them in detail – another welcome point of difference with Chelsea.

Conceptual show gardens are a particular feature of Hampton Court, with designers flexing their creative muscles to create more avant-garde gardens – offerings have explored challenging themes such as homophobic hate crime, landmine injuries and breast cancer. In recent years, the Small show gardens (currently known as Summer gardens) have explored literary themes to good effect.

Should the July weather be less than kind, there are plenty of undercover exhibits to mosey around. Clocking in at over 6750 metres square, the **Floral Pavilion is the** mother of all marquees and like a village flower show gone mad. The immaculately ordered displays of flowers and plants are a unique fusion of art and nature and a testament to the growers' dedication to the pursuit of perfection. With displays from top nurseries like Fibrex Nurseries, Avon Bulbs, Hardy's Cottage Garden Plants, there is quite literally a world of plants to admire, from alstroemerias to alliums, fuchsias to ferns, hostas to hardy bamboos, and cacti to carnations.

The Show's annual rose festival is a sumptuous, sensuous celebration of the flower that defines the British summer, with delectable presentations from top rose growers like Harkness, David Austin, and Peter Beales. The festival is a chance to get acquainted with new rose cultivars, as well sink your nose into some fragrant old favourites.

Lovely as the show gardens are there's no denying that horticultural themed retail therapy is also high on most visitors' agendas – and in terms of quantity and quality, Hampton Court Flower Show takes some beating. As well as the nursery stands there are exhibitors selling everything from the gardening nuts and bolts like decking, fencing and fruit cages to desirable 'lifestyle' products and fancy ornamental extras like weather vanes and sundials. The show's carnival atmosphere makes it all too easy to get carried away, but why not? The sun's shining, the jazz band is striking up, the Pimm's is delicious and that bespoke Italian water-feature would look just fabulous in your garden…

www.rhs.org.uk

A gold-medal garden at Hampton Court

Michelle Duxbury's design for a show garden at HCFS was accepted while she was a student at Capel Manor College (see p.34). One of a group of gardens themed around Shakespeare's comedies, Michelle's garden took *The Merchant of Venice* as its inspiration.

Using grasses such as *Stipa tenuissima*, and *Anemanthele lessoniana* to evoke Venice's watery cityscape, Michelle avoided a literal depiction of water. The garden did feature small, hidden pools planted with *Equisetum hyemale* which, much to Michelle's delight, became a pop-up nursery for damselflies and mayflies for the duration of the show. Three gondola shaped planters (representing the caskets from which Portia's suitors must choose) were freighted with appropriately colour themed plants, including *Achillea milleforum* 'Terracotta' and *Coreopsis grandiflora* 'Sunray' in the gold casket, *Berkheya purpurea* 'Silver Spikes' in the silver and *Cerinthe major* 'Kiwi Blue' and *Agapanthus* 'Northern Star' in the lead casket.

Both budget and preparation time were in short supply. Michelle submitted her design in January and to cut down on costs many of the plants were propagated from seed at Capel Manor, being sown at intervals to ensure that enough would be at their best for the show. Specialist company Linepost supplied the bespoke stripy punting poles, between which were hung muslin banners bearing Shakespeare's words of advice for Portia's would-be suitors. Moved by the breeze, the banners echoed the rippling grasses, evoking the washing lines of Venice transported to an English garden.

Blazing hot summer weather, and a total absence of shade made installing the garden an appropriately Shakespearean labour of love and Michelle had to erect a gazebo to keep the plants from wilting. Although described by Michelle as a 'love it or hate it' garden, the judges loved her original design, its meticulous execution and the fact it stuck to the brief (very important at RHS shows). The garden won gold and best in category – an auspicious start to Michelle's new career as a garden designer.

www.michelleduxbury.co.uk
www.linepost.co.uk

H Hampton Court Palace Gardens

You've got to hand it to Henry VIII, he certainly knew how to think big. When not wreaking havoc on the monasteries or dispatching wives, he was busy collecting palaces. Hampton Court was just one of dozens acquired in his lifetime, and the one most closely associated with his mercurial monarch.

Conveniently sited by the Thames, Hampton Court Palace became a favourite honeymoon destination for Henry and he expanded its already lavish accommodation with no expense spared. Very much the sporty type, the king kitted out his favourite palace with tennis courts, bowling greens

and a tiltyard for jousting – as well as a 750 acre park for deer hunting on his doorstep. Henry's tiltyard lives on in name, home to a 'family friendly' café and subdivided into several smaller gardens including a rather municipal style rose garden and a herbaceous garden with pretty spring borders. In 2009 Henry's 'Privy' (private) garden was recreated in the Chapel Court to commemorate the 500th anniversary of his ascension to the throne. With its green and white stripy fences and brightly painted heraldic beasts, the garden looks authentic and its simple beds are planted with a selection of the plants available to Tudor gardeners, such as lavender, violets, hollyhocks and roses.

The Tiltyard Rose Garden

Subsequent monarchs put their stamp on Hampton Court – Charles II romantically followed in Henry's footsteps by honeymooning here with Catherine of Braganza (more pragmatically, he also installed one of his mistresses in special lodgings at the palace). The 3/4 mile Long Water Canal was dug was for the king and, as a gift to his new bride, Charles planted an avenue of lime trees to flank it – a historic vista that was restored in 2004, with a new planting of 544 lime trees alongside the canal.

But it was the arrival of a new dynasty that really ushered in the biggest changes at HCP. Joint monarchs William III and Mary II enthusiastically developed the palace when they came to the throne in 1689 – commissioning Christopher Wren to add a fashionable baroque palace to the existing Tudor one and creating new gardens quite literally left, right and centre. The Great Fountain Garden (see p.127) was laid out along the East Front of their new palace – in their day it consisted of a 13-fountain parterre. Today it retains its original 'patte d'oie' (goose's foot) shape and radiating spokes of topiarised yews, although over the years these have grown into giant mushrooms. Presumably retained for historical rather than aesthetic interest, the somewhat incongruous formal flower beds dotted around the perimeter are a remnant of the garden in Victorian times. The one remaining fountain punctuates the central avenue, its plume of water drifting on breezy days to sprinkle unwary visitors. Even the Broad Walk herbaceous border along the East Front is on a palatial scale – in the summer a majestic sweep of phlox, delphiniums, dahlias, sweet peas and sedums.

Over on the South side of the Baroque palace, the new monarchs installed a new Privy Garden featuring the latest in continental garden design. Thanks to a major restoration in 1995 William and Mary's Privy Garden today appears as it did in 1702 – a 3-acre essay in full-blown formal gardening. Key design elements are the four plats of gazon coupé (turf cut with intricate patterns picked out in fine sand) and the carefully orchestrated topiary that adorn them. Control freaks will love this style of horticulture, others may find its regimented approach disturbing. The approach is certainly a labour intensive one, with a team of gardeners continually at work trimming edges, tweaking weeds and grooming the gigantic hornbeam bower. Seasonally changing – and historically accurate – bedding displays inject colour, warmth and scent into the glacial layout. Between June and September the

Privy Garden and its terrace host a display of tender plants such as aloes, agaves, lantanas and citrus trees – as they would have done in the 18th century. An ardent plantswoman, Queen Mary housed her collection of tender exotic plants from around the world at Hampton Court, overwintering them in specially constructed 'stove houses'. An unashamed demonstration of wealth and power, Mary's vast collection included 1000 orange trees – a none too subtle reference to the House of Orange, the Protestant dynasty to which her husband belonged.

Continuing along the southern side of the palace, two 'pond gardens' (see below) take the form of sunken flower gardens, with pretty displays of spring and summer bedding – in spring a colourful confection of hyacinths, tulips, bellis and primulas, giving way in summer to tagetes, fuchsias, pelargoniums and nicotiana. Their water features are a reminder of the gardens' origins as Henry VIII's fishponds. The nearby 'Tudor' knot garden looks the part, but is in fact a 20th-century design – its recent restoration to Ernest Law's original 1924 plan perfectly illustrates Hampton Court's multi-layered history. The Great Vine has witnessed many of the changes since being planted by Capability Brown in 1768. It is now the oldest and largest vine in the

The Pond Gardens

world. Housed in a specially built glass house, this gargantuan plant still produces up to 320 kgs of sweet black grapes a year, its remarkable vigour perhaps assisted by generous dressings of manure.

Of course, most people come to HCP to get lost in the famous maze. Originally planted in 1690 as part of the Wilderness garden, the maze survived Capability Brown's tenure as Royal Gardener to become Hampton Court's most visited attraction. Every year some 330,000 visitors navigate its green corridors, taking an average of 20 minutes to reach the centre. Like its namesake at Ham House (see p.117), the Wilderness is anything but wild. It was designed as a place to wander in private, with tall hornbeam hedges, secluded benches and winding paths – the ideal place for romantic encounters. In spring the Wilderness is an enchanting vision of massed daffodils and narcissi and clouds of cherry blossom and magnolia flowers. Although there is a separate charge for the maze, this part of the garden has free entry and is a perfect destination for a relaxed stroll, and a picnic.

The formal gardens (to which there is an entrance charge during British summer time) cover some 60 acres – horse drawn carriage rides are available if the legwork gets too much. The gardens' development over the centuries is charted in a small exhibition, which shows the changing layouts and also includes some beautiful botanical drawings by members of the Hampton Court Florilegium. Even at Hampton Court time doesn't stand still and in addition to the historic gardens, there's also a 20th-century garden, which is used as a training ground for apprentice gardeners. It's a little more rough-and-ready than the immaculately tended main gardens but is a good place for a quiet picnic on a crowded day.

Hampton Court Palace Gardens
www.hrp.org.uk
Summer open: Daily 10.00-18.00
Winter open: Daily 10.00-16.30
The Wilderness, Tiltyard and Rose gardens are open all year round 7.00-20.30 (summer); 7.00-18.00 (winter)

Top-right: William and Mary's Privy Garden,
Middle-right: The Great Fountain Garden, with topiarised yews and Wren's baroque palace in the background. Below-right: The maze

This page and opposite: Pergola, Hampstead Heath

The Hill Garden & Pergola

It's not every back garden that can accommodate an 800ft long pergola, but then the Hill Garden is not your usual kind of back garden. Commissioned by soap magnate Lord Leverhulme and designed by Thomas Mawson, this impressive brick, stone and timber structure was to be the defining feature of the gardens laid out behind The Hill, Lord Leverhulme's capacious Hampstead home. Today the Hill Garden and Pergola is managed by the City of London Corporation. It has been open to the public since the 1960s, but still retains the aura of a private, somewhat melancholy, secret garden.

Built in stages between 1905 and 1925, the Pergola exudes the confidence and opulence of the Edwardian era with its Italianate styling, spectacular scale and commanding position overlooking Hampstead's West Heath. Thousands of wagon-loads of earth contributed to the Pergola's domineering height (over 15ft above the natural lie of the land), provided from the Northern line extension, which by happy coincidence was being built at the same time. Canny businessman Lord Leverhulme even received a fee for taking the soil he needed to build his project. After the war the elaborate, zig-zagging structure fell into disrepair but it was restored in the mid-1990s.

Mawson was a prolific garden designer and a leading exponent of the Arts and Crafts garden (the style took its name from his influential 1900 book *The Art and Craft of Garden Making*). Calling himself a 'landscape architect', Mawson took his lead from Humphrey Repton and stressed the importance of linking the garden to the wider landscape with gradually lessening degrees of formality. It's an approach that can be seen at the Hill Garden where the untamed heath and wailing sirens of the city lie beyond the garden's encircling iron railings and chestnut palings.

Resting atop its red brick plinth (which prosaically housed garden stores and the like), the Pergola consists of a majestic avenue of classical stone columns supporting wooden beams, punctuated by timber 'domes' and 'tents', as well as a stone belvedere. Assorted wisteria, clematis, roses, hops and vines wind their way tenaciously around the columns, providing colour, scent and interest for much of the year. Tucked into the angular folds at the base of the Pergola is a Mediterranean style garden featuring wall-trained fruit trees, magnolias, drifts of euphorbia and sage, gravel paths and giant terracotta pots, an aromatic herb garden, and a box parterre. At the western extremity of the pergola lies a pleasant expanse of gently sloping lawns, plantations of mature trees and shrubs, and an orderly lily pond (built in 1963 on the site of a tennis court). Generously provisioned with benches, this little known Hill Garden is the perfect spot for a romantic picnic or quiet afternoon away from it all. With no dogs allowed, its a perfect place to enjoy one of life's most sensual pleasures – running barefoot on newly mown grass.

The Hill Garden and Pergola
Inverforth Close, off North End Way, NW3 7 EX
www.cityoflondon.gov.uk
Open: Daily 8.30am until dusk

Horniman Museum & Gardens

A South London institution for over 100 years, the Horniman Museum was founded by Victorian tea tycoon Frederick Horniman with the intention of 'bringing the world to Forest Hill'. This popular local museum continues to do just that in the 21st century with Horniman's extraordinary collections of anthropological artefacts, musical instruments and natural history specimens still firmly at its core.

The museum's gardens have always been a popular part of its family friendly identity and boast an original 1903 bandstand, fine views of the South Downs, a small animal enclosure and London's first wildlife trail, which follows a ½ mile stretch of the original Crystal Palace Railway line. A valuable local green space, the gardens also form part of the Green Chain, a wider network of green spaces across SE London.

A recent £2.3 million refurbishment programme has linked the gardens more closely to the museum collections, creating imaginative new display gardens which showcase medicinal and food plants, and plants whose fibres are used to make textiles and musical instruments. As part of the new scheme, the Arts and Crafts style Sunken Garden has been replanted with a colour-coordinated display of dye plants and a Sound Garden has been added to the bandstand terrace. The improvements to the garden combined with the charm of the museum, make the Horniman a great place for the avid gardener to bring the family while also getting a crafty horticultural fix...

Horniman Museum and Gardens
100 London Road, Forest Hill, SE23 3PQ
www.horniman.ac.uk   T: 020 8699 1872
Museum open: Daily 10.30-17.30
Garden open: Mon-Sat 7.30-sunset, Sun 8.00-sunset
Admission free (except for the Aquarium)
www.greenchain.com

Opposite, clockwise from top left: The 'insect hotel' inspection, Grade II listed Victorian cast iron Conservatory, Sunken Garden. This page: Art Nouveau clocktower by architect C. H. Townsend

I # Inner Temple Garden

The High Border

This 3-acre site, overlooking the Thames, could hardly be more historic, having been in cultivation since at least the start of the 14th century and with its first recorded Head Gardener having been appointed as far back as 1546. Over the centuries the garden has taken many forms, from productive medieval orchard to Tudor 'knott' garden to formal parterre. In its time it has weathered all kinds of threats from the great storm of 1703 to the 1987 hurricane. The current garden consists of an unfussy sweep of lawn studded with specimen trees, and a double avenue of 19th century plane trees running parallel with the river along the 'Broad Walk'.

Glorious as its historic 'bones' are, it is the garden's magnificent mixed borders that attract attention today. The High Border, which flanks the elegant iron railings to the north of the garden, has been transformed by Head Gardener Andrea Brunsendorf into a flamboyant mixed border using shrubs, perennials, annuals, climbers and bulbs to create year-round interest. At its radiant climax in late summer, the border pulsates with strong, contrasting colours that are able to stand up to the uncompromising red brick backdrop of Crown Office Row. Bold planting combinations here might include *Dahlia* 'Bishop of Landalff', *Helenium* 'Wesergold', *Aster frikartii* 'Moench', with fiery highlights of *Tithonia* 'Torch', woven through with clumps of *Calamagrostis* 'Overdam' (variegated reed grass). The lofty blue spires of *Echium fastuosum* are a magnet for bees as well as providing emphatic punctuation in the border, while the *Dahlia imperalis* (tree dahlia) is Andrea's pride and joy, and quite possibly the only outdoor flowering specimen in the country. Preparation for the next year's High Border display starts even as the herbaceous plants are being cut down in the autumn, with Andrea's meticulous planning and artistry going to ensure a seamless succession of colour and interest,

Top right: Mediterranean bed; Centre right: Dahia 'Bishop of Landalff' with Helenium 'Wesergold'; Below right: Calamagrostis, Achillea and Dahlias

Andrea Brunsendorf

with spring bulbs yielding to tulips and alliums underplanted with aquilegias, followed by tender bedding. Self-sown poppies, *Verbena bonariensis* and Scotch thistles (*Onopordum acanthium*) grow where they will, ensuring things don't look too regimented. In winter stately grasses, cardoons and pretty early flowering *Rosa banksiae* lend seasonal elegance to the border.

The Mediterranean beds, on either side of the steps down to the lawn, have also been spiced up. In June they are in full swing, their predominantly silvery grey palette studded by strategic dabs of colour. The scope of the planting here in fact extends well beyond the actual Med, with tender exotics like *Salvia confertiflora* from Brazil, *Leontis leonurus* from South Africa and *Dasylirion quadrangulatum* from Mexico. Pink and white roses are the ostensible mainstay of the War of the Roses Border (according to Shakespeare, hostilities began in 'Temple Garden'). In spring however it is massed ranks of tulips that make a pre-emptive bid for glory in this bed, presenting a different colour scheme every year. And when the tulips fade, their ranks are replaced with a vibrant carpet of annual bedding beneath the warring roses.

Tucked away on the other side of Paper Buildings, the Peony Garden is a tranquil space, slightly separate from the rest of the garden. Here the colour scheme is pastel hued, with a ghostly *Wisteria sinensis* twining around the railings and blowsy herbaceous and tree peonies putting on a brief display in early summer. Seasonally changing displays of pots brighten the steps of Kings Bench Walk and the circular pond, the latter providing a shady spot to show off aquatic and marginal plants like gunneras, irises and papyrus sedge. It is here also that Andrea is able to indulge in her unexpected newfound passion for begonias, developing an extensive collection of specimens such as *Begonia luxurians* (the palm leaf begonia).

Since her appointment in 2007 – and she is the first woman to hold the post as Head Gardener – Andrea has set about reinvigorating the 'Great Garden' with some élan. As well as revamping the borders, and steering the garden away from

any municipal tendencies, one of her priorities has been to improve the organic content of the garden's free-draining alluvial soil. To this end, 40 or so tons of horse manure are imported each winter – no easy task given the twin challenges of the congestion charge and the slender dimensions of the service entrance. The garden has too many high-maintenance and mildew prone roses to be completely organic but it is managed with concern for the environment – propagation of annual bedding reduces 'plant miles', and a wildlife friendly native hedge has been planted by the work area. Andrea's permanent staff of two and team of enthusiastic volunteers are supplemented by Boris the spaniel and Hunter the cat, both of whom provide chemical-free pest control.

Another innovation has been a mass planting of 14,000 *Liriope muscari* bulbs, for naturalistic spring colour along the Broad Walk – these pretty 'turf lilies' tolerate the dry shade beneath the plane trees. Future challenges include the creation of a woodland garden underneath the walnut tree, and Andrea has also got her sights set on revamping the King's Bench Walk border, possibly as a proper English herbaceous border.

In the 19th century, under dynamic Head Gardener Samuel Broome, the garden became a venue for a series of chrysanthemum shows, as well as being used by the RHS for its Spring Shows until 1911, when the event moved to Chelsea. Appropriately, under Andrea's energetic stewardship, this connection with the RHS has been revived with a September Floral Celebration being held in the Great Garden in 2008. Day-to-day the garden is a private haven enjoyed by the students, barristers and benchers of the Inner Temple but it is normally open to the public every weekday between 12.30-3pm. In addition, the garden opens for the NGS scheme and Open Garden Squares Weekend, as well as hosting a highly popular rare plant fair.

Inner Temple Garden, EC4Y 7HL
www.innertemple.org.uk
Access to the garden is via the north gate opposite
Crown Office Row
www.ngs.org.uk
www.opensquares.org

Japanese Kyoto Garden

J

An unexpected outpost of Japan in Holland Park, Kyoto Garden was built by the expert gardeners of the Kyoto Garden Association as a gift to Kensington and Chelsea by the Kyoto Chamber of Commerce. This tranquil space opened in 1991, in time to celebrate the Japan Festival held in London the following year, and has been providing a soul-soothing counterpoint to the hyperactive sportiness found elsewhere in the park ever since.

The garden is designed as a traditional *kaiyu-shiki* or 'stroll' garden. Stroll or 'excursion' gardens developed in Japan in the Edo period (1603-1867), when travel inside Japan was restricted and its grounded grandees took to making gardens in which they could take 'excursions' without the need for travel. Such gardens took the form of a symbolic tour through Japan, with features such as rocks, waterfalls, lakes and meadows standing in for aspects of the country's forbidden landscapes.

Although on a more modest scale than most native *kaiyu-shiki* , the Kyoto Garden ticks most of the genre's boxes. Features include a circular path winding its way around the garden, a noisy waterfall cascading down a rugged terrace to represent steep mountain gorges, while the pond with its islands and neatly constructed pebbly shoreline evokes the ocean's mighty expanse. Peacocks – white as well as the usual blue – strut across the grass and sip water from a stone wash basin (*chozubachi*) fed by a bamboo spout while ducks and colourful koi carp patrol the waters of the pond. Other traditional features include picturesque stone lanterns (*toro*) dotted around the garden, a *shishi-odoshi* (bamboo animal scarer) and carefully placed boulders.

Nothing happens by chance in a Japanese garden – be it a dry gravel garden or a ceremonial tea garden – and the Kyoto Garden's planting scheme is as nuanced and considered as its hard landscaping. In its striving to create the essence of a natural landscape in a garden setting, the *kaiyu-shiki* has some affinities with the classic English landscape garden of the 18th century (see Chiswick House and Garden p.60). As in English landscape gardens, trees play a vital role in creating rhythm and texture within the design and, for a small space, the treescape of the Kyoto garden is particularly satisfying. As you would expect, cherries are well represented, with varieties including 'Ukon', 'Kanzan' and the Tibetan cherry *Prunus serrula*; spring blossom is also provided by the native Japanese magnolia (*Magnolia kobus*). The carefully sculpted conifer collection includes Scots, Weymouth and Bhutan pines, their vertical accents balanced by soft mounds of evergreen shrubs such as choisya and box. In spring rhododendrons, irises and azaleas inject vibrant colour into the tasteful scene, while fiery acers (*Acer palmatum* 'Senkaki' and *Acer rubescens* 'Rosie') maintain the heat in the autumn months. Skilful design and specialist care ensure that the garden looks good whatever the season. Every few years a team of gardeners flies over from Japan to make sure the trees and shrubs are pruned correctly. Comprehensive renovations take place every 10 years, the most recent having been completed in the summer of 2011, to celebrate the 20th anniversary of the garden's installation.

Holland Park, Ilchester Place, W8 6LU
Open: daily from 7.30 until 30 minutes before dusk

K Kensington Roof Gardens

The Roof Gardens in Kensington have been a lofty London landmark since they opened in 1938. Over the years they have been known by a number of names; for some, they will always be 'the Derry Gardens' or 'the Derry and Toms Roof Gardens', in reference to the department store for whom they were originally designed by landscape architect Ralph Hancock. For many they are simply 'the Kensington Roof Gardens' while for a brief, brilliant moment in the 1970s they were 'the Biba Roof Gardens', when the famous fashion house took over Derry and Tom's sleek Art Deco premises. Today they are glamorous again, in their current incarnation as one of Sir Richard Branson's 'Virgin Limited Edition' retreats, and are open to the public when not closed for private events.

Occupying a 1½ acre expanse that most London gardeners can only dream of, the Roof Gardens were the biggest in Europe when they were built. Although they were designed to outshine the roof garden at rival department store Selfridges, the Derry and Toms' gardens took their cue not from London but from New York, where Ralph Hancock had created a 'Garden of Nations' on the 11th floor of the Rockefeller Centre in the 1930s. Hancock certainly set a high standard, creating eight gardens including examples of the Japanese, Spanish, Dutch and English styles, as well as a bird sanctuary and a 'sky-scraper vegetable garden'.

D&T's chairman, Trevor Bowen, commissioned Hancock to make something similar in Kensington and was rewarded with a garden that comprehensively knocked Selfridges' into a cocked hat. In London Hancock restricted his thematic palette to a Spanish, a Tudor and an English Woodland Garden, but at 100 feet above pavement level, the logistics remained formidable. The roof was waterproofed with a thick bitumastic base, followed by a layer of rubble for drainage and topsoil for planting. Artesian wells were sunk beneath the

neighbouring Barkers department store to provide the copious water supply required and Derry and Tom's service lift was kept busy hauling materials up to the 6th floor.

Hancock made life a little simpler for himself by re-using several elements from his Rockefeller scheme – the barley twist columns in the Spanish garden's arcades and the sequence of 'stone' arches in the Tudor garden were concrete casts of their American forebears. But with more space to play with in London, Hancock was able to go to town in other ways. The D&T's Spanish garden had not just one loggia but three, as well as a campanile, and a court of fountains, while the English woodland featured a cascade and a river running the length of the roof, overlooked by a tea pavilion. A full-on planting scheme complemented the hard-landscaping with over 500 varieties of trees and shrubs, and annual deployments of thousands of bulbs and bedding plants, the latter produced in the gardens' own roof-top nursery.

Today the gardens are protected by Grade II* listing while the trees have been under a preservation order since 1976. Head gardener David Lewis arrived on the scene in 2007, and immediately oversaw a major renovation, working with historians and RBKC council to take the gardens back to their 1930s glory. As the English Heritage listing does not cover the planting, the gardeners have kept to the spirit of the original design rather than attempt exact historical accuracy.

In the Spanish garden David has taken his inspiration from a 1957 photograph showing a vividly coloured planting scheme. The result is a riot of hot hued dahlias, crocosmia, penstemon, daylilies and gladioli that blaze amid the permanent planting of Mediterranean stalwarts such as olive, juniper, palm trees and yuccas. In the Tudor garden David has opted for a cool black and white scheme that harks back to the Biba era, when the shop ran its own gin-fuelled after hours 'gardening club' for the staff. As a nod to the Tudor theme, this area does not feature any Australasian or American plants (the ghostly pale, night-scented nicotiana being the exception that proves this rule). The Woodland garden remains true to its 1930s self and to this end the lawn has been enlarged to make the stream more visible and replacement liquidambar and elm specimens have joined the mature pollarded English oak, American red oak, limes and mulberry trees that remain from Hancock's original planting. A favourite haunt of the resident ducks and famous flamingos, the woodland garden is magical in spring-time with carpets of snowdrops, anemones and bluebells, and has just been added to the Woodland Trust's list of designated 'bluebell woods'.

Hancock probably didn't design them as such, but his gardens have turned out to be eco-friendly before their time, keeping the building below cool, and reducing run off. Today, David and his two part-time gardeners run the gardens without using chemicals and grow as much as possible from seed in the still extant nursery area. Compost is made on site, while a wormery – fed with scraps from the restaurant kitchen – generates liquid plant food. Pests such as vine-weevil – the almost inevitable corollary of container gardening – are controlled by nematodes, and the ducks take care of the slugs. Sadly, the artesian wells have gone, but water usage in the gardens has been halved by mulching, careful plant choices, and hand-watering. The gardens also do their bit to keep the food miles down in the 7th

floor Babylon restaurant with the planters producing fresh herbs, salad leaves, courgettes, tomatoes, rhubarb and asparagus for the kitchens.

Over the years the gardens have been known as a hang-out for celebrities as various as John Gielgud, the Rolling Stones and Princes William and Harry. They are also a haven for wildlife, attracting several varieties of bees, a regular gang of green finches, and a heron, who comes to call whenever the stream is stocked with fish. The flamingos are defiantly exotic visitors, but have been a signature feature of the gardens for decades; in the Biba era they were joined briefly by a troupe of penguins. As a further incentive for the local wildlife, a meadow of native grasses and wildflowers has been installed on the restaurant terrace in 2012.

Alongside the innovations, David keeps the gardens in touch with the spirit of its past in fun ways such as his quarterly gardening club, which recalls Hancock's 'Horticultural Halls' at the Rockefeller as well as Biba's hedonistic gardening group. Today's equally sociable members enjoy exclusive opening of the gardens, talks and demonstrations, as well as a discount in the restaurant. Thrice yearly charity openings (for Open Garden Squares, Open House Weekend and Virgin's own nominated charity) continue the roof gardens' long tradition of philanthropy.

Apparently designed with an intended lifespan of no more than 10 years, the Roof Gardens celebrate their 75th anniversary in 2013. Their continuing appeal is a testament to Hancock's vision and skill, an achievement that was celebrated by a commemorative plaque that was unveiled at the gardens in January 2012 – the first of its kind to honour a gardener.

The Roof Gardens
99 Kensington High Street, W8 5SA
www.roofgardens.virgin.com
T: 020 7937 7994

Meet The Gardener

As the man in charge of London's best-loved roof garden, head gardener David Lewis is well qualified to advise would-be aerial gardeners. Following Hancock's fearless approach to rooftop gardening, David's top tip is 'If you want to grow something, just try it, even if other people tell you it can't be done! If it doesn't work, it's only a plant, and it won't have cost you a fortune.' Working within the tight framework of a listed, historic structure, David relishes the creativity that this stimulates. A career in advertising predated his switch and retraining as a garden designer, a move that has been vindicated with his landing one of the most sought after jobs in horticulture. And the best thing about working at the Roof Gardens? 'Working in a unique place with the most fantastic team of people.' David not only enjoys free rein at the Roof Gardens, he also gets to look after the gardens at another Virgin Limited Edition retreat, the stunning Kasbah Tamadot in Morocco with their regular gardening team. Some gardeners have all the luck...

Livery Company Gardens

With a history stretching back to Saxon times, the City of London's livery companies are a remarkably enduring feature of the Square Mile.

These ancient guilds represented all the great trades and crafts of the day from apothecaries to woolmen (and even gardeners, whose own guild was incorporated by Royal Charter in 1605). The guilds acted to enforce standards as well as being educators, running a system of apprenticeships. Today philanthropy is their primary activity, and their ranks have been swelled by modern liveries representing the likes of Information Technologists, Security Professionals and Tax Advisors. Those Livery Halls that survived the Blitz or were rebuilt post-war, have found profitable second lives as upmarket venues for hire, whilst still fulfilling their time-honoured role as a meeting place for their members and governing 'Court'.

Among the 40 existing livery halls in the City, 10 lucky ones still have gardens, an asset valued as much in the modern day as in the medieval era when they were used for a variety of activities, from the homely (clothes drying, growing fruit and flowers) to the recreational (strolling and bowling). Today the bowling alleys and greens may be long gone, but the pleasure principle lives on. The three livery gardens listed below are happy to share their precious green space with visitors.

The Salters' Garden

The Salters are one of the twelve oldest Livery Companies in the City but their hall is one of the newest, a crisp white concrete number built in the 1970s to a design by Sir Basil Spence. The garden is newer still, having been designed by David Hicks in 1995, to commemorate the 600th anniversary of the Salters' Company. Bounded on the southern side by a high section of London's Roman wall and to the north by the white walls of the hall itself, this subterranean garden was designed to be seen from above, from the 6th floor balcony of the Salters' Hall (although the public can enjoy a similarly elevated view of it from the St Alphage Highwalk). With its hornbeam, box and yew hedged compartments, plashing fountains and elegant arrangement of York paving, gravel paths and lawn, this is a knot garden in the modern style. Clematis scramble up the iron obelisks and roses ramble over the pergolas in the summer, although the restricted light of the canyon-like site mean they are rather leggy specimens. Each cocooned within a leafy hornbeam enclosure, the garden's wooden benches are the perfect spot to enjoy some peace in the heart of the city.

Salters' Garden
Salters Hall, Fore Street, EC2Y 5DE
Open: Mon-Fri 9.00-17.00

The Goldsmiths' Garden

Salters' Garden, viewed from St Alphage Highwalk

The Goldsmiths' Garden

Like the Salters, Goldsmiths are one of the Great Twelve Livery Companies of the City of London, receiving their Royal Charter way back in 1327. Their magnificent hall, on Foster Lane – the third on the present site – was built in 1835 but the first reference to a Goldsmiths' garden dates from 1495. Their current garden is a more recent affair, with its origins in the destruction and turmoil of the Blitz. Situated on the corner of Gresham and Noble Streets, this two-level garden was formerly the site of the church of St John Zachary, which burnt down in the Great Fire. In 1940 incendiary bombs devastated the area once again and the following year fire watchers from Goldsmiths' Hall began to develop the bomb site as a garden. These prototype guerrilla gardeners created such a flourishing space from the rubble that the Goldsmiths' Company set up a competition for the best bomb site garden in the City, which 'their' garden promptly won five years in a row.

In 1957 the garden was redesigned by Peter Shepheard and refurbished in 1994/5, with a further replanting in 2003. A manicured lawn and central fountain form the soothing focal point of the lower garden, with benches stationed at the foot of the perimeter walls. Avian visitors are equally well provided for, with feeders, nesting boxes and natural perches provided by roses, magnolias, climbing hydrangea and Chinese Virginia Creeper. The scarlet bottlebrush blooms of *Callistemon citrinus splendens* add vivid summer colour to this pared down planting scheme, as do the bedding plants on the cantilevered façade of the Nicholas Grimshaw office building that overlooks the garden. On street level the garden is dominated by two London plane trees with a serene, predominantly white and green, planting scheme featuring hydrangeas, *Anemone blanda*, hart's tongue fern and sweet box (*Sarcococca*). The resulting garden offers a formal but lush green space to escape from the noise and chaos of the City.

Goldsmiths' Garden
Gresham/Noble Street, EC2
Open: Daily, all day

The Barber-Surgeons' Garden

Like the Salters' garden, the Barber-Surgeons' garden is situated in the lee of the Roman wall, although with the added glamour of the remains of an early 4th century defensive bastion. Informal lawns studded with specimen trees, including a foxglove tree (*Paulownia tomentosa*), tulip trees (*Liriodendron tulipifera*) and a yellow *Magnolia* 'Elizabeth' (planted to commemorate the Queen's Golden Jubilee in 2002) make up the bulk of the garden but it is the herb garden that is perhaps of most interest.

Built in 1987, on a derelict bomb site by the Barbers post-war livery hall, this petite physic garden is divided into 45 beds demonstrating the use of plants in medicine from ancient times to the modern day. The selection ranges from aromatic herbs such as meadowsweet and lavender to plants such as yew and liquorice with a proven modern pharmaceutical track record. The planting scheme also includes herbs like parsley, comfrey and spurge that were recommended by John Gerard, the celebrated 16th century surgeon and author of the eponymous Herbal, who became Master of the Barber-Surgeons' Company in 1607. A descriptive list of the all the plants can be found in the garden or alternatively on the Barbers' Company website.

The strange mound behind the curved wall that partly encloses the herb garden is a grisly reminder of the area's history. Buried beneath are thousands of pieces of skeleton from plague pits and churchyards in the area, as well the surgeons' dissecting rooms which once stood on this site. Open to the public but notably bench free, the garden is usually sparsely populated, making it a good choice for quiet picnics.

Barber-Surgeons' Garden
Off London Wall/Wood Street, EC2
Open: Daily, all day

This page: Barber-Surgeons' Garden
Opposite: Goldsmiths' Garden

L London Plants

Over the centuries London's seemingly unpromising terrain has nurtured a surprising variety of plants and even given its name to a few along the way.

Rosebay Willowherb

A colourful opportunist, this once scarce upland plant owes at least some of its current ubiquity to the two world wars of the last century. Its tall, purple-pink flower spikes flourished on forestry sites newly cleared for the war effort of WW1, but it was the Blitz that turned rosebay willowherb into an urban phenomenon. With the disturbed and burnt ground of London's bomb sites providing ideal germination conditions for its wind-borne seeds, rosebay willowherb appeared there in sudden, purple profusion during the summer of 1941. Its Latin name is *Chamerion angustifolium* but to many Londoners it is simply 'fireweed' or 'bombweed'.

Rosebay Willowherb

London Rocket

An immigrant species, despite its misleading common name, *Sisymbrium irio* hails from the Mediterranean. It was known to be flourishing in London by the mid 17th century, but the plant's fortunes waned from the early 19th century until 1945, when it was rediscovered growing near the Tower of London. Specimens of this yellow-flowered annual can still be spotted on the London Wall at Tower Gateway but urban botanists will need to be alert to the presence of the similar looking Eastern Rocket (*S. orientale*), which grows on the Wall at Noble Street, and its hairier relation, the helpfully named False London Rocket (*S. loeselii*), which has naturalized in a few sites in the city.

London Rocket

London Plane

London Plane

Synonymous with the capital's parks, garden squares and tree-lined streets, this is another 'London' plant that botanically speaking is nothing of the kind. Its precise lineage is debatable but it is probably a cross between the eastern and western species of plane, originating in Spain sometime in the 17th century – hence its Latin name *Platanus x hispanica* (although it is also sometimes referred to as *Platanus x acerifolia*). Recognisable by its leathery palmate leaves, its flaking bark, and its furry seed heads, London's signature tree is also remarkably long-lived and can grow up to nearly 50 metres high.

Berkeley Square is home to some venerable London planes, which are among the oldest in London having been planted in 1789 by Edward Bouvier, a resident of the square. They include one tree whose amenity value has been calculated at £750,000, making it Britain's most valuable tree – and a canny investment by Mr Bouvier, had he lived to see it. Other notable specimens are 'Barney', a 17th-century London plane on Barnes Common whose girth measures 8 metres, and the Richmond Riverside Plane, which is thought to be London's tallest London plane. Planted in 1931, the London

plane outside the Dorchester Hotel is a newcomer by comparison but, elegantly illuminated at night, it has become a much loved landmark on Park Lane, and it too has been designated a 'Great Tree of London'.

Resistant to drought, pollution, pruning (expert or otherwise), compacted soil and high winds, the London plane is often regarded as the perfect urban tree. But after some 300 odd years at the heart of city life, it is facing a worrying new threat from Europe – Massaria, a fungal infection that seems to target plane trees. By 2010 around 200 trees in London's Royal Parks had been affected and in March 2011 a branch from a tree in Highbury Fields provided the first formal ID of the disease in Britain. Massaria attacks the upper side of individual branches, making them susceptible to sudden breakage – a bitter irony for a tree that is revered for its reluctance to shed branches (hence its popularity as a street tree). The disease poses a real challenge to cash-strapped councils as trees will need to be inspected frequently and close-up, with the additional expense of platforms or tree climbers. But the good news is that the disease doesn't seem to affect the health of the tree as a whole and can be contained by early identification and bough removal.

Deptford Pink

This now rare wild flower, *Dianthus armeria,* owes
its name to John Gerard, who in his 1597 *Herball*
described it growing in 'the great field next to
Detford (sic)'. At the risk of ruining a lovely story,
it's possible he may have actually meant a different
plant, *Dianthus deltoides,* but Gerard's mistake has
been Deptford's gain. If you want to grow your own
Deptford Pinks, seeds are available from specialist
wildflower nurseries.

Deptford Pink

London Pride

A cheerful cottage garden plant, *Saxifraga x urbium*
is tolerant of both shady and dry conditions. It
flourished on London's bomb sites after the Blitz
and was immortalized by Noel Coward's patriotic
wartime song of the same name, penned in the
summer of 1941. Coward's lyrics picked up on the
plant's ability to thrive almost on thin air:
There's a little city flower every spring unfailing
Growing in the crevices by some London railing' .

London Pride

Haringey Knotweed

This is a 'new to science' hybrid of two notoriously
thuggish plants – Japanese Knotweed (*Fallopia
japonica*) and Russian Vine (*F. baldschuanica*). It was
discovered in 1987 growing on Railway Fields Nature
Reserve, off Green Lanes, by botanist David Bevan.
Haringey is still the only place in the UK to harbour
a wild population of its eponymous knotweed, more
formally identified as *Fallopia x conollyana*.

Haringey Knotweed

London Fruit and Veg

Gone are the days when 'Battersea bundles' meant freshly cut asparagus from the fields of Wandsworth, or the herbalist-surgeon John Gerard could praise the quality of Hackney's turnips, but remnants of London's market gardening past live on. Short's Gardens (WC2) remembers the Mr Short who once rented a market garden there, while 'Cellini', the aniseed flavoured dessert apple raised in Vauxhall in 1828 by nurseryman Leonard Phillips can still be found growing in the area today, at Lambeth Walk Open Space Community Garden, next to Roots and Shoots (see p.188). An even older variety, the scarlet dessert apple Fearn's Pippin, was raised sometime before 1780 in the Fulham garden of one Mr Bagley. Popular in Victorian times, this apple has recently been planted in a number of London school orchards as part of the Fruit-full Schools project.

In the 20th century the John Innes Institute, based in south London from 1910 to 1967, developed several new fruit varieties as part of its research into plant breeding and genetics. Easily recognizable by their 'Merton' prefix, the apples include Merton Charm and Merton Beauty, as well as the Award of Garden Merit winning Merton Worcester (released c 1950) and Merton Knave (released 1975) – the latter two can be seen in the orchard of Fenton House (p.94). Other, quite literal, fruits of their labour include the Merton Gage, the Merton Pride pear and the Merton Bigareau cherry. The Institute's decades long research into apple breeding also resulted in the 'Malling-Merton' (MM) rootstocks, a joint venture with the East Malling Research Station to develop rootstocks with woolly aphid resistance. Two of these, the MM106 and the more vigourous MM111, are still widely used today.

Orchard at Fenton House

'Fresh', 'local' and 'sustainable' may seem like contemporary consumer buzzwords but when it comes to ticking eco-friendly boxes, 17th-century Londoners beat their modern-day counterparts hands down. Back in the day, a swathe of market gardens in outlying riverside villages such as Chelsea, Battersea, Wandsworth and Bermonsdey, as well as eastern suburbs like Hoxton and Hackney, kept the hungry city daily supplied with a seasonally changing menu of fruit and vegetables.

Market gardening took off in England in the 1600s, galvanised by Dutch and Flemish immigrants who were escaping religious persecution. These green-fingered, commercially savvy newcomers bought with them improved vegetable varieties and a talent for optimising the soil's productivity, using techniques such as hot beds to defy the vagaries of the British climate. Proving the adage that where there's muck there is indeed brass, intensive manuring was the key to their success and a neat reciprocal trade evolved with Thames barges carrying fresh produce towards city markets such as Newgate Street, Leadenhall and Spitalfields, and those travelling in the opposite direction piled with horse manure and human 'night soil'. With around 725,000 inhabitants in 1760, London's population must have kept the appositely named Dung Wharf, near Puddle Dock (as shown in John Rocque's 1767 map of the city), busy.

Poor grain harvests in the late 1500's and the newly fashionable trend for eating vegetables meant that market gardening, although by definition a small-scale enterprise (cultivation by the hoe as opposed to the plough), could be a nice little earner. In 1605 the Worshipful Company of Gardeners (see p.260) was founded as an (ultimately unsuccessful) attempt to regulate the burgeoning trade. In 1670 a charter formalised the fruit and veg trade that had grown up by the Duke of Bedford's house in Covent Garden, paving the way for it to become in the 19th century the capital's main produce market. Different areas became famed for particular crops – according to the 18th-century author Daniel Lysons' *General View of the former and present state of Market Gardens*, Battersea was synonymous with fine asparagus, Twickenham with strawberries, while Deptford was a notable producer of onion seed. Evidently veg plots were considered as attractive then as they are today. The Neat House Gardens beside Millbank also doubled up as a kind of pleasure garden, where city dwellers like Samuel Pepys (who recorded several visits), might stop and buy a melon, or simply enjoy a wander.

London's rapid growth throughout the 18th and 19th centuries pushed market gardening further out of town. Today, the trade continues in pockets of Surrey, Kent and Essex, with some producers selling their wares at London Farmers' Markets, where stallholders are kept as local as possible, typically within a radius of 100 miles.

Allens Gardens

Market gardening itself has however made a surprise re-appearance in Hackney courtesy of Growing Communities, a not-for-profit social enterprise dedicated to creating a more sustainable and resilient food system. Their three, organically certified urban market gardens, located in Clissold Park, Springfield Park and Allens Gardens, produce virtually zero-carbon salad leaves for the organisation's veg box scheme. Volunteers help grow the crops, guided by a full-time grower, and at Springfield Park and Allens Gardens visitors can follow a self-guided tour on days when work takes place on the plots. Volunteering is a hands-on way of learning about urban, organic growing but even a site visit is educational, with display boards explaining the niceties of crop rotation and interesting compost heaps and propagation techniques to explore. With productive space at a premium, Growing Communities is also harnessing the potential of small, previously neglected patches of land in Hackney through their Patchwork Farm scheme, in which trained apprentices raise food for the box scheme on micro-sites such as churchyards and back gardens.

Of course, compared to the thousands of acres of local market gardens that once kept Londoners' supplied with their five-a-day, this initiative is small fry, but Hackney's soil clearly still has what it takes: in 2011 the GC gardens produced around 80kg of salad every week, the yields being equivalent of 28.1 tonnes per hectare per year.

www.growingcommunities.org

M Medicinal Garden (RCP)

With its origins stretching back to the reign of Henry VIII, the Royal College of Physicians is the oldest medical college in England. Housed in suitably distinguished quarters – an elegant, Grade I listed Modernist slab by Sir Denys Lasdun and a collection of adjacent white stucco Regency houses – this venerable institution also has a well-endowed garden.

Although a garden has been in place here since 1965, it was replanted with a medicinal theme in 2005. Its seven distinct zones offer a fascinating rummage through the global medicine cabinet, from the 'muthi' plants of traditional South African medicine to the herbal remedies used by native North Americans, as well as modern plant-derived drugs like Tamiflu and Taxol (the former from the star anise shrub, the latter from yew).

Laid out primarily as an ornamental garden, rather than the geometric order beds you might expect from a traditional physic garden, the College garden nevertheless packs in the medically relevant

specimens and contains over 1,000 different plants, all clearly labelled. The Arid Zone beds feature medicinal plants from dry climates such as yellow flowered *Senna corymbosa* (the source of the purgative Senakot) and the architectural *Aloe vera*, whose soothing juice can be used as a treatment for burns. In the Far Eastern bed the Chinese fan palm, *Livistona chinensis* is another elegant plant that is used as herbal medicine by the Chinese and valued in western medicine as a tumour inhibitor.

At the front of the college, the World Medicine beds feature a selection of medically valued plants from around the world, including apparently humble specimens like *Vinca major*, the blue flowered greater periwinkle, which turns out to have a medical application reducing blood pressure. Over in the European and Mediterranean beds one can find the blues beating *Hypericum perforatum* (known to many as St John's Wort), and plants from the Classical world such as the sedative Mandrake (*Mandragora officinarum*), and the pomegranate (*Punica granata*). The pomegranate tree is frequently featured in classical mythology and widely revered for its medicinal properties; its fruit appears on the College's coat of arms. Not all the plants are entirely beneficial to human health – the leaves of the cycads in the Arid Zone beds cause Parkinson's and dementia if eaten, while the toxic alkaloid derived from Monkshood (*Aconitum carmichaelii*) has a deadly application when used as an arrow poison.

As well as showcasing medical plants, the garden is also liberally stocked with plants whose names honour famous physicians, including mythological ones such as Paeon, doctor to the ancient Greek gods, whose name lives on in the peony. Pedanius Dioscorides, the first century Greek author of *De Materia Medica*, a medical encyclopedia that was used as a reference until the middle ages, is immortalised in *Acanthus dioscoridis*. Appropriately, many of the illustrious doctors memorialized in plant names were also pioneering botanists: the *Lobelia* is named for the botanist Mathias de L'Obel, who was also James I's physician while Nicholas Monardes, the Sevillian physician-cum-botanist, gave his name to *Monarda*, or bergamot. Hippocrates, the father of Western medicine, is honoured here by a magnificent plane tree, *Platanus orientalis subsp. Insularis* which dominates the main lawn. This flourishing specimen is supposedly a descendant of the very plane tree under which Hippocrates taught his students on the island of Cos.

The eight parterre gardens in front of the Regency terraced houses of St Andrew's Place take their cue from the *Pharmacopoeia Londonensis*, a medical book published by the RCP in 1618. The *Pharmacopoeia* laid the foundations for the Culpeper's famous *Herbal* of 1652 (originally published as *The English Physician*) and cemented London's role as the centre of plant-based medicine. Each of the gardens contains plants authorised for use by the *Pharmacopoeia* – some like roses and marigolds were valued for the medicinal properties of their flowers, others for their bark, seeds, roots or fruit. The gardens are planted accordingly, thus House 5 (the Pepys Garden) contains plants such as sedum and yarrow whose leaves were used

medically, while House 3 contains plants like peony, marshmallow and angelica whose roots had a medical application. This appealing octet of gardens shows that charm and utility can be achieved in the urban front garden, as well as harking back to the College's Tudor days, when it rented a garden by its premises in the City for the purpose of growing medical herbs.

Royal College of Physicians
St Andrew's Place, NW1 4LE
www.rcplondon.ac.uk

M Myddelton House Garden

It's been a long time coming, but after years of decline and almost as many of restoration, Myddelton House Gardens are finally back on the horticultural map. Something of a shrine in horticultural circles, the gardens – the life's work of revered plantsman E A Bowles – re-launched in spring 2011, following a major Heritage Lottery funded restoration project.

Edward Augustus ('Gussie') Bowles died in 1954 but his presence is very much alive in his garden and many of the rare and unusual plants he raised here are still in situ, such as the enormous *Wisteria floribunda* grown from seed by Bowles and planted in 1903. The current team of gardeners, led by dynamic young Head Gardener, Andrew Turvey, work in the spirit of 'Mr Bowles' (as they respectfully call him), an approach which embraces Bowles' playfulness such as the use of plastic plants in a difficult to reach spot which recalls the artificial apple mischievously placed by 'Gussie' in his fruit bowl. Similarly Bowles' fondness for recycling architectural salvage as garden ornament has been continued in recent introductions such as the 'pre-loved' large stone spheres in the arboretum and the stately metal benches on the pond terrace which originally graced a park in Leeds.

Born in 1865, Bowles was destined for a church career but the deaths of two siblings curtailed his studies and bought him home to Myddelton where he spent the rest of his life collecting and breeding plants and developing the gardens. Although self-taught, Bowles led a distinguished horticultural career and was awarded the Royal Horticultural Society (RHS) Victoria Medal of Honour in 1916, and served as an RHS Vice-President from 1926 until his death. His clout in the gardening world can be gauged by the huge number of plants bearing his name – *Erysimum* 'Bowles Mauve' and *Carex elata* 'Aurea' (Bowles' golden sedge) being among the most well known. Bowles in turn named plants after his friends and neighbours, and he was responsible

for numerous plant introductions including the still widely available Crocus 'Snow Bunting'. After his death, Bowles's famous two-pronged gardening fork and plants from the garden were taken to Wisley to create a living memorial, 'Bowles Corner'. A recent addition to Myddelton has been a reciprocal 'Wisley Corner', an area of the garden previously overgrown with Snowberry and Aucuba. The corner contains plants with Wisley in their name, since Mr Bowles devoted much of his time to RHS Wisley and its development. Bowles's influence spread through his writings and his trilogy about Myddelton, starting with 'My Garden in the Spring', remain classics, while his handbook on his passion, Crocus and Colchicum, became the standard reference book on the species.

Extending to some 8 acres in total, the gardens follow the layout created by Bowles and while there are visitor maps and interpretation boards available to help with navigation, this is really a garden for exploring at will. Although known as the 'Crocus King', Bowles was skilled at raising all sorts of plants in the scant, dry soil at Myddelton and he created a garden with year round appeal. In early spring there are snowdrops, hellebores and daffodils to enjoy, followed later in the season by a National Collection of Dykes Medal winning Iris, recently replanted in chronological order to show the development of the

Iris over the years. The lavender colour flowers of the *Pawlonia tomentosa* (Foxglove trees) are another spring feature. The Tulip Terrace was traditionally planted with tulips to coincide with the celebration of Gussie's birthday on 14 May, an occasion he dubbed 'the tulip tea'. Tulips are used less today due to the attentions of the squirrel population.

The sloping alpine meadow – inspired by Bowles' plant hunting holidays in the Pyrenees – is carpeted in spring with snowdrops, snowflakes and crocus, which give way in summer to a blue haze of wild geraniums. The sheer diversity of Bowles' horticultural interests means there is a world of variety in the garden – visitors in June can admire the glowing red lantern flowers of the *Crinodendron hookerianum* from Chile, inhale the heady scent of *Philadelphus coronarius* 'Variegatus' (syn. 'Bowles' Variety'), or recoil from the carrion-scented, flowers of *Dracunculus vulgaris*, a pungent British native. In July Cape fuschsias and a variety of bottle brush, burst into vibrant flower, showcasing the readiness of plants from hot countries like South Africa and Australia to settle in Britain. The national flower of Chile, *Lapageria rosea*, grows up the clinker wall of the old conservatory and other exotics include *Bauhinia corymbosa* (the orchard vine) and the Taiwanese *Tetrapanax papyrifera* (also known as the 'Rice Paper Plant').

The garden's mature trees, many of them planted by Bowles, generate microclimates invaluable for the tender specimens but the garden is also packed with less rarified, self-sown plants like aquilegias, hedge garlic and *Smyrnium perfoliatum*. However, Bowles' plant choices were not always wise and the Japanese knotweed he admired for its architectural qualities is now feared and reviled as an invasive alien species. Two towering clumps of it – supported within metal frames – have been retained as a cautionary gardeners' tale.

161

Foliage interested Bowles as much as flowers, a line of enquiry that resulted in the area known as 'Tom Tiddler's Ground', which features variegated plants. The gold and silver colour scheme reminded Bowles of a children's game whereby a 'Tom Tiddler' protects his 'ground' from those who would steal his 'gold'. Another strangely named part of the garden is 'The Irishman's Shirt', which turns out to be a diamond shaped brick pillar attached to a wall. Bowles acquired the pillar from nearby Gough Park and had a wall and summerhouse built to keep it company – like the Irishman who asked for a shirt to be added to his solitary button. The 'Lunatic Asylum' also requires explanation, being Bowles' name for the bed where he kept his 'demented' plants – those exhibiting unusual variations such as the corkscrew hazel, yellow-berried yew and Hedgehog holly.

Surprises abound at Myddelton. At the centre of that most English of garden features – a rose garden – stands a romantic centrepiece, the old stone market cross from Enfield Town, rescued from demolition by Bowles and recently conserved. The adjacent 'Pergola Garden' comes into its own in late summer/autumn with its swags of grape vines and autumnal hues. A classic year-round feature is the carp lake developed by Bowles as he wasn't allowed to grow aquatic plants in the New River, which at that time ran through the garden. Giant rhubarb still grows by the margins of the lake as it did in Bowles' day, but this section of the river was closed and filled-in after Bowles' death in the 1960s, its course is now traced by an arching green ribbon of lawn.

Refreshingly for such a historic site, Myddelton is not set in aspic – since Bowles gardened here for many decades the garden can't be returned to a particular moment in time. The current team always ask themselves 'what would Mr Bowles have done?' but have been able to move things forward without offending the soul of the garden. The Heritage Lottery Funded restoration project has resuscitated the once derelict Kitchen Garden,

restoring the potting shed and Bowles' original wooden cold frames – where Bowles kept his collection of rare crocuses and cultivated new hybrids. The Peach House, of which only the wall remained, has been rebuilt from scratch after the original footings were discovered intact beneath the soil. A lean-to glasshouse adjoining the potting shed has also been recreated, and contains a temperate and hot house as well as a vinery and a sunken glasshouse. The overgrown land has been cleared using pigs so that it can be returned to productivity, with beds for cut flowers, vegetables and fruit. The trio of porkers proved very effective and even succeeded in finding some of Bowles' original metal plant labels, missed by the metal detectors. Andrew Turvey really has the bit between his teeth and despite the huge workload elsewhere in the garden has already started to reclaim the totally overgrown Rock Garden, which was the first part of the garden developed by Bowles. Working as much as an archaeologist as a gardener, Andrew and the team have uncovered three original pools and plants such as Purple Toothwort are beginning to reappear as this lost garden is cleared.

Preserving the ethos and ambience of Myddelton House Gardens has been central to the restoration project and even the new visitor facilities in the old stable block have been developed with 'Gussie' in mind. The tea room recalls Bowles' fondness for afternoon refreshment in the English tradition while the plant sales area ensure that, as in Bowles' day, visitors won't go away empty handed. The small museum tells the Bowles story, puts the garden into context and includes a fabulous pair of newly restored 18th-century lead ostriches, which used to grace the garden as ornaments. Its wilderness years over, and with a dedicated and enthusiastic management team behind it, Myddelton House Gardens is once again a must-see on any garden lovers 'to do' list.

Myddelton House Gardens
Bulls Cross, Enfield, Middlesex, EN2 9HG
www.leevalleypark.org.uk   T: 08456 770 600

The choice of plants available to gardeners today might appear seemingly limitless but whilst there's certainly no shortage of companies wanting to sell us plants, the range is not in fact as abundant as it once was. The whims of horticultural fashion plus the demise of many small-scale plant breeders has spelled the disappearance of many once readily available cultivated varieties. It's a loss not just for gardeners, but also for garden historians, pharmaceutical botanists and plant breeders themselves, since a large gene pool is vital for breeding the drought, pest and disease resistant plants required in the climate-changed future.

National Plant Collections are one response to this plight. Set up by the conservation charity Plant Heritage, there are now over 650 such collections across the country, each one a 'living library' dedicated to a particular group of plants. Anyone can be a collection holder, from botanic garden to local authority, from commoner to Queen (and just to prove it, the Royal Household in London has the national collection of *Morus*, or mulberries).

The capital is home to several other collections – West Ham Park holds two, *Liquidamber* and *Trachelospermum*, while Regent's Park's

This page: Eccleston Square, SW1

collection of *Delphinium elatum* hybrids with the RHS AGM can be seen near the Jubilee Gates. Myddelton House (see p.160) holds another very specific group of plants – the Iris Dykes Medal Winners. The superb soil and microclimate of Eccleston Square supports the national collection of *Ceanothus*, with some 60 different varieties, including *Ceanothus* 'Marie Simon' and C. 'Snow Flurries'. This award-winning garden square opens for the NGS (see p.264) and for the Open Garden Squares Weekend (see p.170) and is well worth a visit. Although its openings don't coincide with the *Ceanothus* blossom in April, the garden

which is managed by renowned horticultural photographer and author Roger Phillips and tended by Kiwi contractor Neville Capil, boasts an exciting collection of rare and tender plants. Other attractions include southern hemisphere plants such as *Metrosideros excelsa* (New Zealand Christmas Tree) and *Clianthus puniceus* (Kaka Beak), as well as an extensive holding of *Camellias* and climbing, shrub and tender Tea Roses.

www.nccpg.com
www.ngs.org.uk
www.opensquares.org

Lovingly created and tended by residents, the Ockendon Road tree gardens have become something of an Islington landmark. As a certain guidebook might put it, they are 'worth the detour' and taxi drivers and local walkers do exactly that to admire these charming mini gardens, flourishing in the 'pits' of the trees that line the road. The gardens' modest proportions belie their clout, as they are regular 'Islington in Bloom' prize winners and their kerb appeal has even been known to sway prospective house buyers.

Inspired by similar gardens in Holland, the first Ockendon Road tree garden was planted in 1993; by 2004 nearly all 35 tree-pits had been similarly transformed, thanks to the hard work of newly retired Ockie Road residents, Tony Campbell and Julie Davies who decided to extend the concept to the whole street. Salvaged Victorian edging tiles were used to define the new beds and create a better planting depth, with a wooden alternative devised by Tony's wife, Tessa, being used where traditional edging wasn't possible. Keeping the project as sustainable as possible, the 'tree-pitters' preferred planting medium is a home-produced soil-compost mix, with plants being funded by Ockie Road residents (and subsidised by the gardens' prize winnings).

The four prime movers behind the tree gardens are Aida Trabucco and Julie Davies, and Tessa and Tony Campbell, with ad hoc assistance from others in the road. Each garden they create is different – by design and by necessity, as the road's east-west orientation produces one sunny and one shady side. Amazingly in this era of health and safety gone mad, the gardeners have the support of Islington Council, who have even allowed them to extend some of the smaller tree-pits. The council retains responsibility for the street's trees, the majority of which are elderly crab apples, although these are gradually being replaced with a more diverse selection, including gingko, liquidamber, maple, cut leaf alder, and a tulip tree.

The tree gardeners' year starts in May with a buying spree and intensive planting activity; July is the focus of their endeavours as this is when Islington in Bloom is judged and in October the gardens are tidied and bulbs put in for the spring. With the street trees acting as giant umbrellas deflecting rainfall from the gardens below, watering keeps the four main gardeners busy – an intensive job involving buckets and external taps made available by residents along the street.

Tony, Tessa, Aida and Julie are always striving for variety and colour, and their tree gardens can feature anything from rambling nasturtiums and Californian poppies to hebes, dwarf gorse and rustic hollyhocks and one bed is devoted to herbs. Aconite, vinca and cyclamen have proved successful in the shady beds, while the tree gardeners – ever keen to inject a bit of height into their creations – also deploy an array of climbers such as passion flower, honeysuckle, trumpet vine and clematis, as well as an irrepressible perennial sweet pea which fills the main trunk of one tree. Shrubs and perennials are favoured, and feature some unusual choices such as *Oenothera*

Aida Trabucco, Julie Davies, Tessa & Tony Campbell

and *Mimulus cardinalis*. Easy to pinch annuals are too tempting for thieves and other problems have included vandalism, dogs, litter and basal growth from the trees.

By Tony and Tessa's own admission between May and August their own garden might take a back seat while they concentrate on the tree gardens. But despite the work involved, the rewards are great, the tree gardens have injected real personality to the street while also creating an informal focal point for the community. Keen to promote the concept, Tony and Julie happily offer advice for would-be tree-pitters, from plant choices to hard-won practical tips on materials, planting techniques and aftercare.

Ockendon Road, Islington, N1
www.orra.org.uk

Ockendon Road's Tree-Pit Tips

1) Materials: Earth & compost can be sourced for free from neighbours, or skips.

2) Edging: edging tiles are cheap to buy, but often thrown out when gardens are revamped. You might need 15-30 for a tree-pit. Bricks – need fewer than tiles and require less depth. Stones – similar in size to the bricks

Tiles/bricks/stones can be tamped down (with a hammer and strip of wood). Drop in small stones behind/under them to make the fixing stronger. If faced with the spreading base or roots of an established tree it may be impossible to edge all the way round. An alternative is to make a rectangular box using strips of wood, placed level with the surface. These can, if necessary, be anchored into the earth with vertical wooden strips (placed to avoid the roots).

Allow for the earth level to fall. Keep well below the height of the surround and leave a groove for the water. Remember that new planting raises the earth level.

3) Waterproofing:
To stop water running out through the gaps in the edging, plastic strips (lawn edging) can be cut and pushed down.

4) Prepare the bed:
It is likely that the existing 'soil' will be of poor quality, with sand, rubble, bricks and concrete to contend with. Taking great care not to damage the tree roots, and ensuring that they remain moist, you may want to dig out the existing materials to a depth of 6 inches where possible and replace with earth and compost. Suckers coming up from the base of the tree or its roots can be cut back. This should be done cleanly and close to the base.

5) Watering:
This will be the biggest single commitment. In the case of a mature tree – the tree's leaves stop most of the rain reaching the pit, and the tree roots take what they can. For this reason try to achieve a critical mass of plants so that little earth is exposed to the sun. In summer it will probably be necessary to water once a week; in a heatwave, this can be as much as every other day.

6) Organisation:
In any street, much of the effective work is likely to be done by a small handful of people. If a whole street is to be tackled, the hard-core helpers will probably have to take on a number of the 'orphan' beds. Co-operation (e.g. over sharing equipment) and good co-ordination (for example about any watering rota) is essential.

7) Funding:
If a group of beds, or even an entire street, is involved, and if no other source of funds is available, it is probably necessary to have a whip-round. In Ockendon Road we found a number of people happy to offer – indeed most would rather pay than do the work!

8) Problems:
Expect and accept a few minor set-backs, e.g. dog mess, careless individuals and occasional vandals. There may be plant theft too. If so, see what they take and avoid those plants. In general, best not to put in expensive and unusually attractive plants (and remove the price label!)

Tree gardens can feature anything from rambling nasturtiums and Californian poppies to hebes, dwarf gorse and rustic hollyhocks...

O Open Garden Squares Weekend

Paris may have its boulevards and New York its gridiron, but luckily for garden lovers, London discovered years ago that when it comes to town planning, it's hip to be square.

The first residential London square to be developed around a central garden was Soho Square in 1681, following on from the first, gardenless 'piazza' of Covent Garden (1631). With their light, airy properties grouped around a pleasant open space, squares were popular with house-buyers and over the next two centuries dozens were built throughout London, from St Andrew's Square in Kingston to Albion Square in Hackney.

The fashionable garden designers of the day were often called into landscape these desirable new developments, with luminaries such as Charles Bridgeman and John Nash working at St James' Square, Humphrey Repton designing Russell Square, and Thomas Cubitt responsible for the planting of Belgrave Square. As on the great country estates, rustic landscapes were all the rage in 18th-century London, with Portman Square and Grosvenor Square being laid out as 'wildernesses', while Cavendish Square even had sheep grazing on it to conjure a rural idyll. By the mid 18th-century most squares had been enclosed for ease of security and maintenance

and today many remain tantalisingly out of public reach, their leafy interiors glimpsed behind railings and shrubberies and open only to key holders.

One weekend every June, however, something magical happens, when private squares and gardens across the capital open their gates to the public as part of Open Garden Squares Weekend. The event is run by the London Parks & Gardens Trust and has grown from a one-day event with 43 participating garden squares in 1998 to a city-wide extravaganza of over 200 gardens in 2011. Gardens now taking part include well-groomed private squares such as Earl's Court Square and Eaton Square, but also more contemporary creations such as prison gardens, community gardens, therapeutic gardens, allotments, as well as gardens belonging to shops, hotels, hospitals, schools, religious and legal organisations. The atmosphere is festive, with picnicking opportunities aplenty, and some gardens also lay on food, music, children's activities and

plant sales. Following hot on the heels of the fantasy gardens of Chelsea Flower Show (see p.50), the Open Garden Squares Weekend shows off some of London's most private and special 'real' gardens, as well as some of its most historic green spaces.

Open Garden Squares Weekend
www.opensquares.org

London Parks & Gardens Trust
www.londongardenstrust.org

O Osterley Park

The skies above may echo to the relentless roar of airborne traffic from nearby Heathrow, but on the ground, walking through Osterley's gardens, all is serene.

With over 350 acres of grounds to its name, Osterley Park exudes the air of a country estate, complete with a perfectly choreographed Arcadian landscape contained within simple black park railings, and, at the centre of it all, a gracious stately home. The house and its environs assumed their current form in the latter half of the 18th century, when the wealthy Child family began remodelling the existing Tudor mansion into 'the palace of palaces'. With top Georgian architect Robert Adam at the helm, the house was dressed to impress with its statement corner towers, swanky pedimented entrance portico and glacially elegant neo-classical interiors. The grounds too were revamped to complement the house, a task

that involved creating a pleasure garden, a series of lakes and tree planting on a grand scale. Today Osterley's treescape includes a fine collection of oaks, featuring North American red oaks, as well as cork oak, holm oak, and a Japanese Daimyo oak.

Although it's not known who reshaped the grounds, Sarah Child took a keen interest in the garden and Mrs Child's Flower Garden was the first part of the garden to be restored to its 18th century splendour by the National Trust. This part of the garden was strategically placed so that it could be seen from Mrs Child's dressing room and in her day it was planted with the most fashionable plants. The garden is focused around a pretty, semi-circular Garden House designed by Adam, which was used for entertaining and to overwinter orange and lemon trees. Flower beds stud the lawn, and are at their brilliant best from June to September but with attractive shows of

tulips, daffodils and forget-me-nots in spring. Mature trees add a sense of scale and history to the garden, and include a redoubtable Cedar of Lebanon, planted here in 1760 and one of the oldest trees in the garden.

Entertaining and showing off was very much at the core of Osterley's raison d'être and the pleasure garden reflected these concerns. In the same way that the house flaunted the fashionable design and architecture of the day, the garden showcased the latest plants. As its name implies, Osterley's American Garden featured newly discovered plants from the New World, which began to reach Britain in the second half of the 18th century thanks to American plant hunters such as John Bartram. The recent discovery of a list of plants ordered for the garden by Mrs Child in 1788 has paved the way, in 2010, for an ongoing restoration of this part of the garden. Named after a gardener at Osterley in the 1940s, 'Dickie's Border' illustrates the 18th century style of planting in 'height order', whereby tall plants such as *Ilex aquifolium* were placed at the back

of the border, while the shortest such as *Armeria maritima* (thrift) were deployed at the front.

The old Tudor walled garden houses a cutting garden and a vegetable plot. Marigolds, being the symbol of the Child family (as well as excellent companion plants), are well represented here. The Temple of Pan hails from a slightly earlier phase of Osterley's re-development and is the start point for the Outer Pleasure Ground Walk. Its classical portico looks out over the Great Meadow, which having never been ploughed or fertilised, is a vision of wildflowers and grasses in the summer. In April & May, blossom and bluebells are twin attractions at Osterley. But, regardless of season, the parkland as a whole offers lovely walks and picnicking opportunities – proof that the pleasure principle still holds strong at Osterley.

Osterley Park and House
Jersey Road, Isleworth, Middlesex TW7 4RB
www.nationaltrust.org.uk
T: 020 8232 5050

Teahouse, Petersham Nurseries

Petersham Nurseries

Stepping into Petersham Nurseries is like entering a parallel universe – it's light years away from the aesthetically challenged supermarket approach of many garden centres. This aspirational world is one where everything – from humble garden twine to antique wrought iron benches – is carefully selected and beautifully displayed.

Plants are inspirationally arranged in old wine crates on wooden barrows or battered zinc topped tables while inside the vintage greenhouses the relaxed, bohemian vibe continues with colonial-style ceiling fans whirring above and expensively distressed furniture, Sicilian pottery, luxurious bath products and tender exotics like orchids and amaryllis. The hands-on gardener hasn't been neglected either with practical gardening kit including Ilse Jacobsen rubber boots and traditionally crafted tools by Burgon & Ball. For those who like to grow their own from scratch there are seeds by upmarket brands like Duchy Originals, Sarah Raven and Franchi.

Despite its exclusive riverside location (a short walk from Ham House, see p.116) and aesthetic appeal, the nurseries' prices (for plants at any rate) are fairly down-to-earth. You can bring a touch of the Med to your patio with a luscious hot pink *Oleander*, try a bit of prairie planting with a *Stipa tenuissima*, or bump up your herbaceous border with a *Eupatorium rugosum* 'Chocolate' – for under a tenner per plant. The well edited plant list aims to provide gardens with year-round colour and structure and includes seasonal bedding and bulbs, unusual herbaceous perennials and a gorgeously scented collection of old fashioned roses. Trees – ornamental and fruit – are chosen with the smaller urban garden in mind and there is an enticing choice of terracotta pots for container plants.

As if all this wasn't enough, PN is also home to a Michelin star restaurant and a Teahouse, which serves delicious cakes, ethical coffees and speciality teas, as well as light lunches in a more relaxed, garden shed ambience.

The current incarnation of Petersham Nurseries owes its existence to Gael and Francesco Boglione, who live in neighbouring Petersham House and who bought and renovated the nursery, reopening it in 2004. Petersham House itself has a glorious garden (occasionally open to the public – see website), whose 'hedgerow gone mad' 150ft double herbaceous border inspires the stock in the nursery and whose kitchen garden supplies the restaurant with salad, herbs and edible flowers. Petersham House is set within a historic Thames landscape, known as Arcadia, which runs along the Thames from Teddington to Kew. It's a beautiful but sensitive site and visitors are strongly advised to avoid coming by car but instead to visit on foot, bicycle or public transport. The website has details of all the permutations as well as delivery options for purchases.

Petersham Nurseries
Church Lane, Off Petersham Rd, Richmond, TW10 7AG
www.petershamnurseries.com
Nursery: 020 8940 5230   Teahouse: 020 8605 3627
Nursery open: Mon-Sat 9.00-17.00, Sun 11.00-17.00
Teahouse open: Tues-Sat 10.00-16.30, Sun 11.00-16.30

Phoenix Garden

Oasis is an overused word in the context of urban gardens, but it perfectly describes the Phoenix Garden, an unexpected green space hidden away behind the Phoenix Theatre, off busy Charing Cross Road. Surrounded on all sides by buildings, and overlooked by Centre Point, the Phoenix is like a modern day version of a London garden square, albeit with significant differences from its historic cousins.

Run as a communal garden by volunteers, the Phoenix is open to the public 365 days of the year, so it's worlds away from the exclusive key holder only access of some London garden squares. The garden's laid back atmosphere makes it a popular lunchtime retreat for local workers and residents alike, with its handsome wooden benches (some carved with pithy epigrams), and grassy areas offering sanctuary for the world-weary.

Unlike the typical London garden squares, which were a carefully planned element of the city's expansion in the 18th and 19th centuries, the Phoenix sprang into life on the site of a car park, which in itself was a former bomb site. From these unpromising origins, the garden has developed over the past thirty years into a flourishing green space, and collected numerous Camden in Bloom awards in the process.

Sustainability is at the heart of the garden's ethos, with plants being chosen for their drought tolerant qualities and wildlife friendliness. It's a strategy that seems to have paid off – in summer visitors walk amidst groves of foxgloves, drifts of valerian, daisies, euphorbia and geraniums, with the sound of bird song and the thrum of busy bees and hoverflies all around. A couple of ponds provide a suitably moist habitat for urban frogs and fish, while some areas of the garden are left deliberately unkempt to benefit wildlife – brambles, nettles, thistle and teasel all have a place in this garden. The garden's bird population make the most of the collection of nicely maturing trees which form the backbone of the space and which include chestnut, gingko, birch and cherry.

Lovingly tended by its teams of volunteers, the Phoenix is filled with quirky detail and informal planting, which gives it a lively, distinctive personality so often lacking in municipally run gardens. Here, plants thrive in all manner of containers, from concrete tubs to an old wheel-barrow, while the hard landscaping uses all kinds of material from old kerb stones and paving to brick filled gabions. Sinuous paths make the small space seem bigger and in summer blowsy roses in cheery shades of red, yellow and pink punctuate the greenery while exotics like bananas and echiums strike a more tropical note.

Hard work underpins the apparent informality of the garden: its green and pleasant appearance is maintained by two regular volunteer groups, a weekly 'Clean Sweep' team and a twice monthly Sunday workshop group which tackles heavy duty projects like paving and gabion construction. The garden has a community gardener and hosts planting workshops, parties and a popular annual 'agricultural show' with rustic attractions like morris dancing, falconry and farm animals.

The Phoenix Garden, 21 Stacey Street, WC2H 8DG
www.phoenixgarden.org
Open daily 8.30-Dusk

Oasis is an overused word in the context of urban gardens, but it perfectly describes the Phoenix Garden...

P Putting Down Roots

Gardeners come in many unexpected guises, and the volunteer gardeners of Putting Down Roots are no exception, belonging as they do to one of London's most marginalized and excluded communities: the homeless.

The programme is one of the 'Skills and Employment Services' offered by the homeless charity St Mungo's and aims to help clients gain skills and qualifications which will lead to paid or voluntary work. The scheme provides accredited training to NVQ level as well as giving participants the chance to get stuck into real gardening jobs at sites across London for clients such as Bankside Open Spaces Trust and Team London Bridge.

At St John's Church, hard by the busy transport hub of Waterloo, St Mungo's gardeners have transformed a run-down formal garden into an award winning space, with pretty parterre, smart new paths and cheery mosaic decorations. Over in Bermondsey, food production is at the heart of their Melior Street garden, with grown-to-order vegetables being sold to a local restaurant to generate funds. In partnership with the Eden Project, Putting Down Roots gardeners also helped to create the 'edible' Roof Garden on top of Queen Elizabeth Hall in 2011, to celebrate the 60th anniversary of the Festival of Britain.

Although each St Mungo's garden has its own character, a common feature is their abundance of self-seeding plants. Inexpensive fillers, these enterprising pop-ups also bring a welcome unpredictability to planting schemes, as project co-ordinator Jonathan Trustram explains, 'you never quite know where the evening primroses, forget-me-nots and honesty are going to spring up.' It's an hospitable approach to horticulture that reflects the core values embodied by St Mungo's: respect and ambition, excellence and creativity, diversity and equality.

www.stmungos.org

Plant Sale: St John's Church, Waterloo

The Garden of St John's Church, Waterloo

Q Queen's Wood Organic Garden

A rare remnant of ancient woodland, Queen's Wood is a much-loved local nature reserve in north London and a site of considerable ecological importance. Its bosky charms are enhanced by the lively community café (run as a not-for-profit organisation) housed in the old Lodge, and by the organic garden tucked away in what was once the Lodge Keeper's garden.

A team of community volunteers from the Friends of Queen's Wood, co-ordinated by the aptly named Lucy Roots, tends the garden twice weekly in the summer, keeping the café supplied with freshly gathered seasonal herbs, fruits and vegetables and taking home the excess. All manner of veg and fruit fill the raised beds, from Jerusalem artichokes to runner beans and white currants, while the productive areas are complemented by a small shrubbery, a physic bed stocked with medicinal herbs, and a wildflower area.

The produce may be abundant but gardening organically in a woodland glade calls for a firmly defensive approach. Fringed by wildlife friendly ground cover such as ivy, bluebells and herb robert, the garden is a magnet for slugs and snails, pigeons and squirrels – all keen to partake in the harvest. As a result plants are netted to within an inch of their lives with old net curtains being utilised as lo-tech but effective fruit cages. Not all wildlife is made to feel unwelcome though, as the bee hives, hedgehog house and mini-beast log pile make clear. Other eco initiatives include a tidy sequence of compost bins, a leaf pile and solar panels on one of the sheds.

Queen's Wood Organic Garden
(behind Queen's Wood Lodge Café)
42 Muswell Hill Road, N10 3JP
www.queenswoodgarden.org

FEVERFEW

Effective remedy for
headaches and
migraine. Helps with
labour pains.
Applies locally to
relieve irritation from
insect bites and
protects against attack
by flying insects.

R Redcross Garden

Octavia Hill was quite a lady. A co-founder of the National Trust, she was also a pioneering campaigner on behalf of the urban poor, and funded several social housing projects. One of her lasting legacies is this charming garden in Southwark, set out in front of the pretty terrace of Tudorbethan style cottages she built in the 1880s.

With her emphasis on attractive, good quality homes and community space, Octavia Hill's approach to social housing was enlightened, whilst remaining thoroughly domestic in scope. Red Cross Cottages' residents had a community hall – envisioned by Hill as a 'parish parlour' – as well as the garden, which was designed as an 'open air sitting room'. Today, the cottages still provide social housing while the garden has been given a new lease of life as a vibrant community garden, managed by Bankside Open Spaces Trust. Thanks to the efforts of BOST and local volunteers the garden's postwar decline

has been reversed and it has been restored to its Victorian splendour. Serpentine paths, well-stocked borders, a pond and neatly mown lawns testify to a well-loved space and there are plenty of benches on which to sit back and enjoy the tranquil atmosphere. Even on a bleak February day the garden is worth a visit with winter flowering jasmine, hellebores and *Iris sibirica* to cheer the spirits. Visits later in the year are rewarded with colourful tulips, and swathes of billowing ornamental grasses and lavender.

Red Cross Garden
50 Redcross Way, SE1 1HA
www.bost.org.uk
T: 020 7403 3393
Garden Open Daily
Admission free

R RHS Horticultural Halls

Chelsea and Hampton Court Flower Shows may be the RHS's headline events in London but the smaller, seasonally themed shows – held at the Horticultural Halls on Vincent Square – have a particular charm of their own. Perhaps it's the indoor setting: instead of parading through the vast marquees of Chelsea and Hampton Court, visitors admire the floral displays and trade stands in the august surroundings of the Horticultural Halls. Hard by the RHS's Vincent Square headquarters, the Halls provide a weather proof venue with a sense of history – Lindley Hall, with its barrel vaulted glass ceiling, was opened in 1904 by King Edward VII, while the sleek Art Deco styling of the adjacent Lawrence Hall dates from 1928.

Once held every month, shows at the Horticultural Halls are now held four times a year. They start with the London Plant and Design Show in February, followed by the London Orchid Show in March and, book-ending the gardening year are the Great London Plant Fair (March/April) and the London Autumn Harvest Show (October). Visitor numbers are small – only about 5,000 per show (compared to the 157,000 who attend Chelsea) – which makes for a low-key, almost village-like atmosphere, far removed from the fashionable crush at Chelsea.

The autumn show in particular feels like a village hall event that has been miraculously transported to London from the sticks, with plates of expertly grown giant vegetables laid out for inspection with pinpoint precision. A closer look at these disconcertingly perfect specimens reveals an eclectic range of entrants, from Dukes to humble commoners, all fighting it out for a coveted RHS medal. But it's not all elephantine parsnips and obscure heirloom apples, 'pretties' get a look in too with dazzling displays of late flowering plants such as dahlias, chrysanthemums and nerines providing colourful inspiration as summer fades.

Thanks to the shows' small scale and friendly ambience it's easy to meet (and buy from) exhibiting nurserymen. At the autumn show this might mean a chance to chat to no dig guru Charles Dowding about winter lettuce production or get some hot tips (as it were) from chilli expert Michael Michaud. Perfectly timed to coincide with the start of the growing season, the spring Great London Plant Fair is an obvious port of call for those wishing to stock up on bulbs, plants and seeds and get tips from the plantsmen and women who have raised them. RHS Advisors are on hand at all the shows to answer gardeners' questions from pruning dilemmas to pest problems, so there's no excuse for an under performing garden. Visitors will find it hard to leave empty-handed with the cream of UK nurseries and garden traders also plying their wares here.

RHS Horticultural Halls
Greycoat Street and Vincent Square, SW1P 2PE
www.rhs.org.uk

R Roof Garden on the Southbank

The optimistically designated 'Sun Deck' on the architects' original plans for the roof of the Queen Elizabeth Hall has for years been a no-go area for the public because of access problems. But in 2011 something wonderful happened – the arid concrete rooftop was transformed into a garden, commissioned as part of the Southbank's 60th anniversary celebrations of the Festival of Britain.

The pop-up plot featured raised beds overflowing with vegetables, an orchard and a lawn as well as naturalistically planted native trees and wildflowers. The project paid homage to the British love of gardening and the countryside, and regenerated not just the QEH roof, but also the lives of the people who helped install and plant it. Created in partnership with the Eden Project, the garden was built from scratch by volunteers from homeless charities St Mungo's (see p.178), and Providence Row Housing Association. The collaboration has a proven track record having completed several previous gardening projects, including two award-winning show gardens at Chelsea Flower Show (see p.50).

With its own café-bar, mellow vibe and panoramic views over the Thames, the Roof Garden was an instant hit with and enraptured visitors clamoured for an encore. Their wish was granted and in April 2012 the roof garden reopened, thanks again to the skill and dedication of the gardening team, but this time with a more internationally themed planting scheme to celebrate the South Bank's Festival of the World.

Queen Elizabeth Hall
Southbank Centre, Belvedere Road, SE1 8XX
www.southbankcentre.co.uk
www.edenproject.com
www.providencerow.org.uk
www.stmungo.org

This one-acre site in Lambeth is productive in more ways than one: a place where people are nurtured as much as plants. Half the site is given over to the teaching facilities, greenhouses and raised beds of vocational educational charity Roots and Shoots, the remaining half-acre is a flourishing wildlife garden. Even the wooden clad learning centre is eco-friendly with a trio of biodiversity boosting roofs – a large solar one, a green one planted with sedums and thrift and a brown one designed to attract miner bees and digger wasps.

Set up as a charity in 1984 by Linda Phillips, Roots and Shoots offers disadvantaged young people aged 16-21 training in horticulture and retail, as well as environmental education for the wider community. Trainees stay for a year and learn a range of life skills to prepare them for the world of work. The approach is holistic – for example working in the on-site shop improves numeracy and imparts retail and social skills. Placements in high-profile gardens such as Buckingham Palace and the Royal Hospital provide quality work experience. The Roots and Shoots shop incidentally does a roaring trade in its own-produced honey (recently voted the best in London) and 'Orchard Bounty' apple juice. The plants sold here are also well worth buying – raised on site by the trainees, they are acclimatised, sturdy specimens and reasonably priced.

Young people thrive here, as does the wildlife garden. Although a garden had been in place since 1984, it didn't really take off as a wildlife one until 1999 and the arrival of David Perkins, the Wildlife Outreach worker. Under David's care the garden has become a beacon of biodiversity, and is a popular venue for local school groups. Visitors enter through the 'Secret Gate' – beautifully crafted by the handy David from curvy oak planks and reclaimed hinges – and step into another world. In midsummer such is the garden's abundance that it is sometimes difficult to spot the different habitats it contains. The summer meadow is rich with native plants and is only cut once a year – a regime that ensures a healthy population of moths such as little

skipper, common blue and six-spot burnet, multiple species of hoverfly, crickets and grasshoppers. Hard-working honey bees live in an apiary tucked discretely behind a hedge of espaliered Discovery and Egremont Russet apples and there are hand-crafted insect boxes all around the garden, including an insect sized 'Trellick Tower', populated by spider hunting wasps and red mason bees. Appropriately for this hive of activity, Roots and Shoots is also the base for the London Beekeepers Association (see p.24), who hold regular meetings and lectures on the site.

The large pond with reed bed and dipping platform is home to frogs and newts while the romantically named 'William Blake's Paradise Corner' contains two further small ponds surrounded by exotic South American planting. Throughout the garden plants have been chosen to appeal to gardeners as much as the wildlife, and in amongst the self seeded verbascum, fennel and euphorbia are well-established 'Fantin Latour' and 'Graham Thomas' roses and *Hypericum* 'Hidcote'. But although clearly well-loved, it's a far from manicured space

and – tidy-minded gardeners look away now – insect friendly weeds like deadnettles and brambles are often left in situ. Beloved by bumble bees, echiums are a particular feature and their success here reflects the mild microclimate of this sheltered site – one lofty *Echium pininana* specimen reached 14 feet in 2001. Both *E. pininana* and *E. candicans* are now rarities in their native habitats.

Enveloped in greenery and surround-sound insect and bird noise, the garden utterly belies its earlier history as a former industrial site, with oil contaminated soil and strewn with engine debris. The half-acre garden even finds room for a magnificent horse chestnut and oak trees. There are regular public open days – look out for the spring Science Open Day, Apple Day in Autumn and openings for Open Garden Square Weekend (see p.170) and the National Gardens Scheme in the summer (see p.264).

Walnut Tree Walk (off Kennington Rd), SE11 6DN
www.rootsandshoots.org.uk   T: 020 7587 1131

The Wildlife Garden

> # *Young people thrive here, as does the wildlife garden."*

Linda Phillips

St Mary's Secret Garden

Tucked away behind the Geffrye Museum (see p.105), this aptly named garden is a hive of activity. A community garden-cum-horticultural project, St Mary's takes a truly inclusive approach to gardening, aiming to provide a resource for the whole community. This includes the running of accredited horticultural courses for local residents, youth training and therapeutic gardening sessions for those with physical disabilities, terminal illness or mental health issues. Clients, students and volunteers all help to maintain the garden, which local key holders can use at weekends.

A series of interlinking garden areas have been created on the tardis-like 0.7 acre site and, as the whole space is managed on organic principles, it's also something of a wildlife sanctuary as well. Birds, newts and hairy footed flower bees have all made a home here. The woodland garden features wildlife friendly drifts of cow parsley and jack-in-the-hedge, wood piles for mini-beasts, as well as a cluster of bee hives. The bees are managed by the Golden Company – a social enterprise teaching beekeeping skills to young people. A children's bug trail winds through the woodland, and the branches of the trees above reverberate with bird song – a real tonic in this built-up part of London. Other senses are stimulated in the herb and sensory garden, whose raised areas and level paths have been constructed with accessibility in mind, and which bring delicious

herbal aromas within sniffing distance. The garden's bees make full use of the flowers here and in the herbaceous and shrub borders, in return producing honey that is sold at the Golden Company stall at Borough Market and is highly sought after. Raised beds are also a feature of the veg growing area where neat metre square beds ensure easy access to crops for those with mobility difficulties. A new well-being zone is currently being developed; funded by Ecominds, the garden is being built with the participation of people with direct experience of mental distress, and will create a garden for the whole community to enjoy.

The large, fully accessibly greenhouse is the propagation hub of the garden, generating plants for the garden and supplying St Mary's thriving plant sales area. This is a great place to source reasonably priced organically grown veg plants such as salads, tomatoes and beans as well as herbs (either freshly cut or in a pot), seasonal bedding plants and house plants. The shop also sells seeds gathered from the garden, own-made compost and comfrey plant food. The home-made preserves are also really popular and make it almost impossible to leave this place empty handed.

St Mary's Secret Garden
50 Pearson Street, E2 8EL
www.stmaryssecretgarden.org.uk
T: 020 7739 2965
Open: Monday-Friday 9am-5pm

S Seeds of Italy

Ladies selecting & grading seeds, Franchi warehouse, Bergamo, early 1900s.

If you enjoy eating Italian food, why not grow the ingredients yourself? This is the question that north London based 'Seeds of Italy' has helped to answer for many years.

Founder Paolo Arrigo is passionate about growing and cooking fresh regional Italian vegetables and he's keen to convert us Brits to the cause. For some he's pushing against an open door but, sceptics take note, his proposition is not as outlandish as it might sound. With the Alps, Dolomites and Apennine mountains within its borders, Italy has a climate that is more Alpine than Mediterranean and consequently many of its vegetable varieties are easily hardy enough to withstand the British weather (whatever that is these days). The Seeds of Italy catalogue is filled with cold-loving veggies like Radicchio Orchidea Rossa, Alpine Fennel Montebianco, Savoy Cabbage of Mantova, and Snow Pea Taccola Gigante, all of which thrive on these chilly shores.

Seeds of Italy import from 'Franchi Seeds', who are 7th generation seedsmen based in Bergamo. Using a traditional 'commissioning' system, Franchi (pronounced to rhyme with 'chianti') sources over 90% of its seeds from local growers in Italy, rigorously maintaining regional provenance

and quality – if the seeds aren't up to scratch, the whole crop is destroyed. It's a traditional approach that has stood Franchi in good stead since 1783, fostering long-standing relationships (some of their growers have been with them for 3 generations) and making their products a byword for reliability and authenticity. Franchi produce dozens of regional varieties such as Cavolo Nero di Toscana which, Paolo reveals, actually sells better in the UK than in its native land.

Food is at the heart of everything that London-born, Italian-bred Paolo does: the Seeds of Italy story started in the family deli when customers kept asking him to bring back seeds from Italy. Paolo thought it would be fun to have a seed stand at the deli and once he had found a partner in Franchi, the business took off, selling to other delis before expanding to include garden centres and mail order (Paolo makes the interesting point that in Italy seeds are sold where food is sold, not in garden centres). Twelve years on and the Seeds of Italy catalogue offers rich pickings, featuring staples like tomatoes, lettuce, courgettes and pumpkins, as well as flowers and green manures, Italian truffle trees, and fruit such as grapevines and pomegranates. Fig-lovers will be thrilled to discover that there are some delicious Italian alternatives to the ubiquitous 'Brown Turkey' fig, such as the purple-black Brogiotto from northern Italy – perfect for serving with Parma ham.

With the trend for grow-your-own, business is brisk, selling not just seeds but their logical extension – specialist Italian preserving equipment to convert gluts into long-lasting supplies for the larder. Reinforcing the link between growing, cooking and eating, Paolo's cookbook *From Seed to Plate* shows not just how to cook Italian produce but how to grow it too. Italians, Paolo notes, are 'just so' about their food, and this means particular dishes demand exactly the right ingredients: San Marzano tomatoes for passata, Borlotti 'Lamon' for the Venetian speciality 'Pasta e Fagioli', Tonda courgettes from Piacenza for stuffing with the cheese and ham of that region. Even herb varieties know their place in Italian cuisine, with no self-respecting cook using Bolloso Napoletano basil to make pesto – for that you would, of course, use Basilico Classico Italiano from Genova, while the enormous leaves of its Neapolitan cousin are far more suited to wrapping buffalo mozzarella.

So, with the pick of his warehouse at his disposal, what does Paolo grow in his own garden? Like any retailer he tends to use up unsold stock – broken seed packets and short date seeds and so on – but his veg patch essentials include Pea Piccolo Provenzale, Chicory Rossa di Treviso, yellow French bean Meraviglia di Venezia and Tomato Principe Borghese (traditionally used for sun-drying and known as the 'eternal tomato' for its storing qualities). Paolo shares his enthusiasm and knowledge of cooking and growing Italian-style at regular masterclass events and the Seeds of Italy warehouse in Harrow holds several shopping open days where gardeners can buy direct and get expert advice at the same time. With row upon row of tempting Franchi seed packets to choose from, it's the horticultural equivalent of being let loose in a sweet shop. Seedaholics, you have been warned…

Seeds of Italy
www.seedsofitaly.com

Paolo Arrigo

S Sheds

If gardens are a refuge from the world, then sheds are the ultimate inner sanctum; a calm haven where gardeners can shelter from the elements, store tools, pot up seeds, ponder the meaning of life or simply have a quiet brew up. Modestly sized, and of haphazard construction, sheds exert a charm that is inversely proportionate to their architectural status. Even off the peg editions can inspire affection, though only after their brassy orange shiplap planks have mellowed, or been tempered with a lick of paint – the natural state of the shed is picturesque decay. Home away from home for allotmenteers, sheds – be they ramshackle or regimented, practical or playful – unerringly reflect the inhabitants. They are one of gardening's most perfect forms of self-expression.

"*I love London – I don't have a dream of going to the country, I have a dream of escaping into a green London.*" **Paul Richens**

Portability is not usually a requirement when starting up a veg garden but when your 'patch' happens to be in the middle of Europe's biggest construction site it's essential.

Currently residing in the heart of the King's Cross development, the Skip Garden is an innovative project run by Global Generation, an organisation that supports young people to increase their awareness of self, community and the environment. Working with the developers, GG have negotiated temporary leases on sites where building is yet to start, but with the proviso that the garden can, in the words of Garden Manager Paul Richens 'up sticks and move at the drop of a hat' when the site needs to be developed. Created out of 7 old rubbish skips (the ultimate large scale portable growing container), the garden has already moved once, a process accomplished in just 1$^1/_2$ days.

The garden's skips have been ingeniously adapted to provide a variety of growing spaces, including polytunnels and even a mini orchard, using the materials indigenous to building sites: pallets, scaffolding planks, water pipes, and monoflex sheeting. Soil is the imported ingredient here, because of the polluted onsite soil, but it will never need to be replaced as is replenished courtesy of the garden's arsenal of composters, wormeries and comfrey plants – as Paul notes 'that's very cosseted soil in there!'

As well as being used by local businesses (who use it to teach their staff about sustainability), the garden is a resource where local schoolchildren enthusiastically acquire hands-on gardening skills and meet– many for the first time –bees, worms and other garden wildlife. A pair of Portakabins serves as a 'Flying Classroom' where older students take BTECH business and horticulture classes, part of which involves them sharpening their entrepreneurial reflexes by selling the produce they have grown to local restaurants.

Paul Richens

For Paul, born to a long line of food growing Londoners, getting young people to connect with the natural world around them is his reward. For him gardening touches every aspect of being human, 'it's craft, it's science, it's art and it's spirituality – it's a wonderful thing.'

Global Generation
www.globalgeneration.org.uk

S Spring Fever in Kew

Go down to Kew in lilac-time, in lilac-time, in lilac-time;
Go down to Kew in lilac-time (it isn't far from London!)
And you shall wander hand in hand with love in summer's wonderland;
Go down to Kew in lilac-time (it isn't far from London!)

Alfred Noyes wrote these celebrated lines over a century ago, but his recommendation to visit Kew when the lilacs are in flower is still a good one. The current lilac garden was renovated in 1993 and contains over 100 hardy lilac specimens – from early flowering 'Hyacinthiflora' hybrids to the later Series Villosae cultivars. Flowering dates vary each year but an advance telephone call or email will help you ascertain when the fragrant blooms are strutting their stuff.

Of course by the time the lilac gets going, spring is already well under way and from late winter right through to May visitors can saunter through a sequence of massed bulb displays (achieved by lifting large areas of turf, throwing the bulbs on the ground and replacing the turf). Cheerful yellow aconites light up the Holly Walk, signalling the end of winter, and are followed in March and April by a blue mist of Scilla siberica along the Cherry Walk. A carpet of *Crocus vernus* cuts a purple and white swathe between Victoria Gate and King William's temple in March, while the Broad Walk is planted with two Narcissus cultivars to ensure a good show of daffs from February through to May – the aptly named 'February Gold' giving way to fragrant 'Pheasant Eye'. In May the Conservation area around Queen Charlotte's cottage transforms itself into a bluebell wood, giving visitors a chance to see why our native *Hyacinthoides non-scripta* are superior to their Spanish cousins.

For more showy late spring displays head for the Azalea Garden and Rhododendron Dell.

Kew's first Azalea Garden was laid out in 1882 but this current incarnation dates from 1995 and traces the development of deciduous Azalea hybrids from the 1820s to the present day. Its beds are a riot of hot pink, yellow and orange flowers – the perfect way to lift the spirits on a less than kind spring day. Another popular destination at this time of year, the Rhododendron Dell showcases over 700 species, including scented varieties like *R. Kewense* 'King George' and *R. loderi*. It is located in a part of the gardens landscaped by Capability Brown in the 1770s. Unfortunately on my visit this area was out of bounds due to spraying against Oak Processionary Moth – an unwelcome spring/summer visitor to Kew, whose hairy caterpillars seriously damage trees and can cause an allergic reaction in humans and animals. It's a reminder that Kew is not a theme park but a complex entity that, as home to the world's largest collection of plants, requires constant nurturing. A major research and conservation hub, Kew in fact contains 1 in every 8 of the world's plant species, making TW9 the most plant bio-diverse postcode in the world.

Spring and summer is the best time to pop into the Waterlily House – the hottest of Kew's glasshouses. Built like a tiny glass Greek temple, albeit one whose shrine is a circular pond, this is the humid home of giant *Victoria cruziana* waterlilies, whose leaves can grow to 2 metres in diameter. On a larger scale the semi-subterranean Princess of Wales Conservatory also has a pond and 10 computer-controlled climatic zones. It showcases animal as well as plant life with resident piranhas, terrapins, and jazzy yellow and black poison dart frogs (safely behind glass). In the dry tropics section the cactus collection sports a

Syringa vulgaris 'Sensation'

Hanami (Cherry blossom viewing)

gratifyingly high quota of rude shapes, whose spines however emphatically signal 'look but don't touch'. More user friendly plants inhabit the moist tropics and these include banana, pineapple and ginger. The PoW Conservatory is also big on orchids – Kew's huge collection is the oldest in existence and encompasses specimens that flourish in sub-arctic conditions to ones that enjoy basking in the warm fug of a tropical rainforest.

Alpine plants get a glasshouse to themselves, in the award winning Davies Alpine House, which opened to great fanfare in 2006. The arched design of this wacky looking building, coupled with some computer wizardry, creates the cool, dry and windy conditions favoured by alpines (defined as plants growing above the tree line). Displays change frequently and, depending on the time of year, may feature campanulas, dianthus, primulas, saxifrages and thymes or even the rare Chilean Blue Crocus. The nearby Rock Garden is packed with a permanent display of plants with altitude – this 'Pyrenean mountain valley' was built in 1882 and is planted with mountain and Mediterranean flora. Its rugged terrain takes you across six continents in the space of half a hectare, including British natives like Cheddar Pink (*Dianthus gratianopolitanus*) and Cuckoo Pint (*Arum maculatum*). Cascading 'mountain streams' are also a feature of this area.

Spring also sees Kew Palace awakening from its winter hibernation. This 17th-century red brick house was used by King George III and his family and today it is run by Historic Royal Palaces. There's an additional charge to visit the palace, which is open roughly April-September (see www.hrp.org.uk for exact dates), but it's well worth it. The palace has two gardens of its own to explore: a formal parterre with manicured box edged beds and the adjacent 'nosegay garden', which is framed by a magnificent laburnum tunnel.

Royal Botanic Gardens
Kew, Richmond, Surrey, TW9
www.kew.org
T: 020 8332 5655 (visitor information)

The library, SLBI

South London Botanical Institute

The SLBI is an organization in the best British tradition: altruistic, egalitarian and just a little eccentric. Founded over 100 years ago by A O Hume, a retired Indian Civil Servant, the SLBI is dedicated to encouraging and enabling local people to study botany.

The Institute's rather formal nomenclature, with its whiff of worthy Edwardian self-improvement, is misleading. The organisation is in fact very inclusive and friendly, and is open to professional and amateur botanists or indeed anyone with an interest in learning about plants. The well-used education room brims with specimens being scrutinised by after schools science clubs. Annual membership currently stands at £10, for which members get the run of the institute's facilities, including a well-stocked library, a microscope room, as well as a varied programme of evening lectures by distinguished botanists, social events and field trips (excluding travel costs and entrance fees). Members can also get involved with research projects such as the long-running survey of St Leonard's churchyard in Streatham – the findings of which will feed into the *London Flora* currently being prepared. Courses in botanical illustration are run twice yearly and there is often a plant themed art exhibition to admire in the upstairs meeting room. At the heart of the Institutes' resources is the Herbarium, a historic collection of over 100,000 dried plant, lichen, algae and fungi specimens, diligently mounted on card, annotated, and stored in the original black iron cabinets designed by AO Hume. Many specimens are over 100 years old and are an invaluable resource for botanists today. Consisting of several herbaria, the collection, with typical SLBI idiosyncrasy, contains a particularly strong record of Shetland Isles flora.

The SLBI is still based in its original home in unassuming Tulse Hill, the magnificent mature *Gingko biloba* in the front drive perhaps the first hint to the unsuspecting passerby that this is no ordinary Victorian house on Norwood Road. For, in addition to its other resources, the SLBI has the perfect aid to plant study in the shape of its own botanic back garden. Measuring just 24 x 16 metres, it is billed as 'London's smallest botanic garden' but size appears to be no object to its ambition and its neatly labelled beds contain over 500 species. The garden was a feature of the SLBI from its inception, when it was described at a 'living museum of strange visitors'. Today, although none of the original 'strangers' have survived, the garden is packed with interesting specimens from home and abroad, exploring a lively selection of botanic themes.

Visits to the garden get off to a bloodthirsty start in the greenhouse, which is home to a collection of carnivorous plants, a grisly source of fascination particularly for younger visitors. The Australasian bed showcases the extraordinary range of plant life from down under, including 18th century introductions by the plant hunter Joseph Banks such as *Sophora tetraptera* (New Zealand Kowhai), and *Callistemon citrinus* (bottlebrush). Closer to home is the 'weed garden', which flies the flag for British native plants – its label is ironic since these plants used to be regarded as weeds. Over in the Dry Border, Mediterranean plants take centre stage with grey leaved toughies like *Stachys byzantina* (lamb's ears) and *Phlomis italica* specially adapted to reduce evaporation, and succulents such as *Sedum populifolium* which have their own in-house water supply in their fleshy stems. Fragrant plants like rosemary, lavender and sage are also drought resistant but other scented plants are given their own border. This even handedly includes *Iris 'Florentina'* – whose violet scented roots are used in the perfume trade – and its foul smelling relative, *Iris foetidissima*. Medicinal plants are showcased in two borders, one of which is themed around Gerard's Herball of 1596, the other exploring pharmaceutical and medicinal plant remedies.

There is also a choice of poisonous plants in the garden, by way of counterpoint, these include deadly nightshade, aconite and poison ivy. Over by the pond there's a bed dedicated to monocots, an important division of the plant kingdom whose subjects are defined as having only one seed leaf (cotyledon). Monocots include grasses, bamboos and palms, sedges and architectural plants such as *Cordyline australis*, as well as native flowers like *Iris pseudacorus* (yellow flag iris) and later summer flowering South African plants like *Eucomis bicolor* and *Nerine bowdenii*.

Formally laid out and packing a lot of plants into its modest urban footprint, the garden is tended by part-time gardener Sarah Davey, and an assistant, together with volunteer help from members. This verdant plot is a popular venue for plant sales and open days such as the Open Garden Squares Weekend and biannual nettle weekend. SLBI events are famous for the excellence of their cakes; members can also enjoy the garden with a glass of wine on summer 'twilight' openings.

Having celebrated its centenary in 2010, the SLBI is gearing up for another century of inspiring interest in plants and reconnecting Londoners to the natural world, and in particular their local area. Current chairman, (former Natural History Museum botanist) Roy Vickery, is dismissive of the idea that you have to go far out of London to discover plants. His mantra is 'rediscover the local' and according to him, cosmopolitan London is just the place to do that. Enthusiastic about the future of the SLBI, Roy sums up its charms by describing it as a place where 'you can be yourself and you don't have to pretend to be cleverer than you are'. It is nothing short of a south London treasure.

South London Botanical Institute
323 Norwood Road, SE24
T: 020 8674 5787
www.slbi.org.uk
Open: Thurs 10.00-16.00,
other times by appointment

Thames Barrier Park

Not a garden per se, but included here for its dramatic and modern planting, the work of French landscape architect Alain Provost. The park was carved out of a 22 acre, decontaminated, brownfield site on the north bank of the Thames. It was opened in 2000 and affords incredible views of the flood defences of the same name and was the first riverside park to be opened in London in 50 years.

The park's most photographed feature is the Green Dock, a 16 foot deep sunken garden that runs diagonally across the rectangular site. Referencing the area's industrial maritime past, the canal-like Green Dock ripples with undulating topiarised yew hedges. These evergreen tramlines enclose ribbon like paths and a 'rainbow garden' planted with colourful blocks of single species such as iris, perovskia, sedum and lavender. The Dock is topped and tailed by a fountain filled plaza at its entrance and a Pavilion of Remembrance beside the river. It is the park's pièce de résistance, although its impact does depend on the yew hedges being kept in trim and indeed surviving – some are looking a little unwell. Up on ground level, the park's open spaces are divided up by single species stands of silver birch, oak and pine planted in grid formations, with swathes of wild meadow contrasting with crisply mown lawn. Design interest aside, the park's other attractions include a ringside view of the Barrier, a children's play area, basket ball court and a highly rated café.

Thames Barrier Park,
North Woolwich Road, E16 2HP
www.thamesbarrierpark.org.uk
T: 020 7476 3741
Open daily from 07.00 (closing time varies according to season)

T Thrive in Battersea

Long proven as a means of improving physical and mental health, gardening is a remarkably potent and supple therapeutic tool. National charity Thrive harnesses the power of gardening to improve the lives of disabled people and their inspirational work can be seen in action at their project in Battersea Park, where the charity runs three gardens.

Thrive's services are tailored to the needs of the individual clients (or 'gardeners', as they are known), and include programmes for those recovering from strokes or heart attacks, for dementia sufferers, and a transition programme for mental health patients moving back into the community. Young people with special educational needs are also catered for and Thrive run gardening courses leading to vocational qualifications. With the emphasis firmly on ability rather than disability, everyone at Thrive wears the charity's signature purple shirts, an egalitarian policy that makes it difficult to tell therapists and volunteers from gardeners – which is no doubt one of the intentions of the dress code.

At the time of writing Thrive's 'main' Battersea site (prominently sited near the tennis courts) is out of action, pending the construction of a smart new building with workshop, classroom and office space. While that project gets underway, the best place to see Thrive's work is the Herb Garden. This magical plot enjoys a slightly less high profile location, being hidden away in Battersea's staff yard, but it feels pleasantly like a secret garden, and is worth seeking out.

Created in 2000, like Thrive's other gardens it's a socially inclusive showcase for the charity. Visitors are welcome to come and soak up the relaxed, happy atmosphere, see the gardeners at work and interact with them. An elegant Victorian style greenhouse overlooks the well-ordered, abundant herb beds, which are divided into distinct zones, exploring different aspects of these versatile plants, from culinary and dye uses to medicinal herbs. Here also can be found 'surprising edibles' such as day lilies and tulips and global super plants like bamboo. Although the garden is not officially organic, it is managed without chemicals and the plants positively burst with health and their vigorous growth, vibrant blooms and enticing scents make them perfect ambassadors for Thrive. Most of the plants are propagated on site from seed and such is Thrive's high standard of plantsmanship, many of the plants which were used in the charity's prize winning 2010 Urban Garden at Chelsea Flower Show were raised here at Battersea.

Thrive's gardening skills can also be seen at the Old English Garden in Battersea Park, where Thrive works as a contractor. Further afield there are several outreach programmes in London, including Slade Gardens in Stockwell (where the charity has helped set up a community garden) and New Covent Garden market, where Thrive have created a potager.

Thrive
Battersea Park, SW11 4NJ
www.thrive.org.uk

T Topiary

After centuries of falling in and out of fashion, the ancient art of topiary is staging a 21st-century comeback. The practice of clipping evergreen shrubs and trees such as yew, box and privet into interesting shapes goes back to the Roman era and in one of his many letters Pliny the Younger proudly describes the box hedges and topiary sculptures at his villa in Tuscany.

The Tudors were very keen on topiary too with a fondness for intricate knot gardens and fantastical beasts sculpted from living trees. The form went into steep decline, however, in the 18th century; mocked by Alexander Pope and ruthlessly swept aside by the 'naturalistic' vistas of landscape gardeners like Capability Brown. Revived by the Victorians and the 'English Garden Movement' of the early 20th century (Christopher Lloyd's father wrote a book on the subject), topiary became a quirky feature in many a British garden.

In London topiary can most famously be seen at Hampton Court (see p.124), which condenses several centuries of topiary styles into one garden – from the 17th-century yew maze (which, on the express orders of the King, escaped Capability Brown's attentions) to its ancient umbrella-like yews and the recreated Privy Garden. But for all its ancient pedigree, topiary is perfectly suited to the modern small urban garden, providing year round interest and structure with an often humourous twist – animals, trains and even baked goods are all fair game for the topiarist's shears. And there's no need to make like Edward Scissorhands either – established topiary is surprisingly low-maintenance, requiring a trim once or twice a year.

www.topiaryhouse.co.uk
www.topiaryarts.co.uk
www.paramountplants.co.uk

U Underground in Bloom

For an activity whose therapeutic benefits are widely acclaimed, gardening can be a surprisingly adversarial pastime. London's gardeners are no exception, with a long tradition of competitive horticulture – from the 'best bombsite garden' competitions of the 1940s to the annual inter-borough floral combat of London in Bloom.

In recent years London Underground has got in on the act, with stations across the capital vying every summer to see which one has the best hanging baskets, tubs or cultivated garden. The outer stations, which tend to have more available growing space, have been active competitors from the off, but every year more stations take part. These days even some of the spatially challenged central stations take part in the event which had more than 70 entrants in 2011.

The gardens are tended by staff in their spare time but some have more difficult terrain to nurture than others. Hampstead, for example, is the capital's deepest tube station and therefore not the obvious location for a vegetable patch. But – as part of the Capital Growth programme – it developed a well-stocked 'behind the scenes' veg garden that won first prize in that category in 2011 (pipping Brent Cross and Warwick Avenue to the post). Hampstead's street level garden picked up extra 'green points' for its wormery and eco-friendly approach. Judges also assess the positive impact of the gardens on customers and staff. In the same year Bromley-by-Bow was deemed the station with the best hanging baskets, while North Acton's colourful bedding displays picked up the prize for the best cultivated garden. Prizes are awarded in September at City Hall.

Vertical Garden – Athenaeum

Five star hotels are not usually known for their sense of fun but the Atheneaum Hotel on Piccadilly is an honorable exception. Home from home to countless stars of stage and screen, in May 2009 this elegant art deco hotel added 'vertical garden' to its list of luxurious attributes. And not just any old perpendicular garden either but an ambitious 10-storey creation by architectural botanist Patrick Blanc.

Covering some 260 square metres, the Athenaeum's 'Living Wall' wraps around the front and side façades of the hotel, setting up a lively horticultural 'conversation' with the verdure of Green Park on the other side of the road. The hotel's lush tapestry is planted with over 260, mostly rare, species, handpicked by M. Blanc from the world's temperate and tropical climes to suit London's usually mild and humid microclimate. The cosmopolitan selection includes the world's biggest single collection of Urticaceae (nettles) as well as interesting specimens such as *Adiantum capillus-veneris* (the black maidenhair fern), *Fascicularia bicolor* (a hardy bromeliad from Chile whose grey-green rosettes turn a glowing red at the end of summer), and *Fuchsia regia* the so-called 'climbing fuschia', from South Brazil. Also included in the mix is one of Blanc's favourite plants – *Iris japonica*, rated by him for its superb architectural qualities.

Ingeniously planted on an irrigated felt surface, the Athenaeum's lush façade was put to the test just a few months after installation when Britain's capricious climate unleashed one of the coldest winters in decades. A few species turned up their toes in protest – the usually hardy evergreen shrub *Stachyurus salicifolius* for example, did not survive the cold, wet winter but others like the winter dormant *Mimulus* sailed through. One year on from installation, and despite the meteorological hiccup, the garden has flourished and with the winter casualties replaced, the planting has evolved into a decadent, velvety mantle draped over the hotel. In

keeping with the garden's avant-garde credentials, the plants' happy demeanour is produced without the benefit of a traditional growing medium like soil, rather, their daily needs are met by an automatic watering and feeding regime. Pruning remains a physical human intervention however, with plants being cut back two or three times a year.

The Athenaeum's Living Wall is an unusually public spirited private garden – enjoyed not only by its guests and staff but also by anyone travelling up and down Piccadilly. Upper deck bus passengers are privileged by a particularly good view – some compensation for being stuck in stationary traffic. An ecological statement as well as an aesthetic one, the 'Living Wall' thriftily re-uses precious urban space, adding nature and biodiversity to a site where nature has been stripped away by building development. London's birds too have been quick to take advantage of this new landmark, darting over from Green Park to snack on the Wall's plentiful insect population.

The Athenaeum, 116 Piccadilly, W1J 6BJ
www.athenaeumhotel.com T: 020 799 3464

V Vertical Veg

When it comes to growing vegetables in London, it's not always lateral thinking that's required – sometimes the only way is up.

In 2009, when the reality of a 40-year wait for an allotment hit home, Camden resident Mark Ridsdill Smith decided to see what he could grow on his small (9x6ft) north-west facing balcony, and the six south facing windowsills at the front of his house. Surprised by his container garden's productivity, the following year Mark started systematically recording his harvests, and their equivalent supermarket cost, and the Vertical Veg blog was born.

While acknowledging that window box and balcony gardening can never provide all our food, Mark's 2-year experiment does prove it can make a worthwhile contribution to a household's larder, with salad leaves and tomatoes emerging as the most 'valuable' balcony crops. As well as lovingly detailing harvests as varied as strawberries, aubergines and tromboncino squash, the blog is packed with

practical advice for those growing in a small space. Topics include how to re-use compost, where to source your seed and instructions on how to make a 'self-watering' container from a milk carton and a yoghurt pot (sticky-back plastic not required).

Although Mark and his family have recently moved to Newcastle, both balcony and blog continue as an online showcase. Mark is still very much involved in London's gardening scene and is often back in the capital sharing his expertise at training courses on container food growing for the likes of Capital Growth, Garden Organic's Master Gardeners and King Henry's Walk.

www.verticalveg.org.uk
www.capitalgrowth.org
www.gardenorganic.org.uk
www.khwgarden.org.uk

Mark's Vertical Veg Tips

1)   Wood from skips is useful for making containers to size – line with plastic to prolong life and / or use linseed oil as a preserver.

2)   Fruiting plants like courgettes, squash and tomatoes need big pots.

3)   Don't overcrowd a pot – use the spacings on the back of seed packets as a guide.

4)   Good drainage is essential. Check water flows freely out of the bottom when watered. Stand pots on feet if needed.

5)   Use good quality compost. For peat-free options, try New Horizon and Vital Earth multipurpose composts. Fertile Fibre is also a good option.

6)   Municipal compost varies in quality but some is good. It's also cheap and sustainable, so do try it.

7)   Multipurpose composts usually contain enough nutrients for six weeks of plant growth. After that, feeding is needed.

8)   Worm compost is the ultimate container fertiliser. It is high in nutrients and microbial life, and good at retaining water.

9)   To see if your plants need watering, put your hand into the soil, three or four inches below the surface. The soil should feel moist, not dry or wet.

10) Daily attention is the secret of successful container gardening.

Frequent light watering wastes water, doesn't satisfy the plants requirements and leads to a shallow root system more susceptible to drought. Water thoroughly and allow the soil to dry out between waterings.

When you water try and water the soil at the base of the plant and not the leaves, that way the water is more likely to get to the roots.

223

V Volunteers

It's always surprising where plants are able to put themselves. In London self-seeded 'volunteers' can be spotted growing in all manner of improbable and apparently inhospitable locations: protruding out of chimney stacks or sallying forth from minute cracks in the pavement.

London's railway lines are enlivened by spontaneous colonies of the irrepressible butterfly bush, *Buddleia davidii*, which was recently voted 'the plant that best represents London' by visitors to the Museum of London. Buddleias are a London staple, but their aggressive tendencies don't endear them to everyone. Less domineering plants about town include Mugwort (*Artemisia vulgaris*) and Rosebay Willowherb, while cheery cottage garden opportunists like hollyhocks and opium poppies always raise a smile.

London's horticultural landscape also benefits from human volunteers. For those whose gardening ambitions cannot be satisfied at home, volunteering provides a range of outlets for green-fingered activity around the city. There are roles ranging from stewarding in the Conservatory at Chiswick House (see p.60) to administrative posts at the RHS and a raft of hands-on helping opportunities at charities like Thrive (see p.212) and community-based enterprises such as St Mary's Secret Garden (see p.192) and Brockwell Park Greenhouses (see p.228).

This page: Hollyhocks in Hackney
Opposite top: Rowan Vuglar,
Harleyford Road Community Garden

W | Walled Gardens

Brockwell Park, see following page

Ravenscourt Park

Ravenscourt Park

With its rose clad pergola, herbaceous borders, rose beds and crazy paving, the Walled Garden in Ravenscourt Park is very much a period piece. Visitors will see a genteel Edwardian 'English' garden that's world's away from today's informal prairie planting and wild flower meadows.

Originally part of the kitchen garden for Ravenscourt House, the walled garden was re-designed by Lt Col J J Sexby, the LCC's Superintendant of Parks and Gardens, when the grounds of Ravencourt House became a public park in 1888. Its labour intensive requirements proved incompatible with the dwindling council resources of the modern era, and this once cosy corner became increasingly unkempt.

The garden's current well-groomed appearance is thanks to a group of loyal volunteer 'friends', set up by local resident Angela Clarke in 2002. They work alongside the Park's head gardener on the first Saturday of every month. Between 10 and 15 people turn up for each session, with ages ranging from 'oldies' to parents with young children – one four-year old has been coming to help in the garden since before he was born! Having been granted council permission to work in the garden, the enthusiastic volunteers embarked on a war of attrition against the all-pervasive bindweed. As Angela recalls, 'Our first task was weeding, weeding, weeding. All very soul destroying as each month we thought we had made progress, only to be met with just as awful a situation when we returned for our next morning in the garden.' In the end glysophate was used in the rose beds but the bindweed in the herbaceous beds is still a problem requiring hand weeding. Ten years on, the garden is in good shape and the volunteers' work is now largely maintenance – although they are itching to give the herbaceous beds a thorough overhaul. A much-loved sanctuary amid the buzz of the park, the garden looks its best in high summer when the roses and herbaceous beds are in full flower.

www.ravenscourtgarden.btck.co.uk

Brockwell Park

In Brockwell Park, the fortunes of another Sexby designed walled garden have also been revived, as part of an ongoing multi-million pound restoration project.

Like its counterpart in Ravenscourt, the Brockwell Park Walled Garden was created from the former kitchen garden of a grand house – the Regency mansion Brockwell Hall, whose landscaped grounds became a public park in 1892. Sheltering within old brick walls is a popular 'secret' garden, designed like Ravenscourt as a summer garden, replete with colourful roses, fragrant peonies, herbaceous perennials, yew topiary, and a wisteria covered pergola. Overseen by the Park Manager, Paul Carter (who also designs the garden's bedding schemes), the recent restoration has seen the York stone crazy paving and 'rope' edging relaid, the timber Arts & Crafts style garden shelters replaced and over-dominant shrubs and trees thinned out to restore the original sight lines. Volunteers from the Brockwell Park Friends group and the adjacent Brockwell Park Community Greenhouses (BPCG) work with the park's staff to help tend this generously stocked garden. Like its cousin in Hammersmith, Brockwell's walled garden is a Green Flag Award winning space.

www.brockwellpark.com
www.brockwellgreenhouses.org.uk

This page and opposite: Brockwell Park Walled Garden

The lovely thing is that everyone really enjoys their morning in the garden and by working all together we can really see the results of our efforts."
Angela, Ravenscourt Park

The Rose Garden

Westminster College Garden

Clocking in at over 900 years old, WCG is what you might call a historic garden. In the Abbey's past it was a hardworking monastic garden, home to an orchard, fishponds and the all important medicinal herb garden. Today this ancient precinct is cherished as a tranquil oasis in the hubbub of modern Westminster.

The modern knot garden – recently redesigned – references the monk's infirmary garden and has been planted with culinary and medicinal herbs as well as a selection of dye plants. A neat little rose garden, enclosed in a double hedge of hornbeam and box and planted with Rosa 'Gertrude Jekyll' and 'Sceptr'd Isle', commemorates the Queen's Golden Jubilee and recalls that Westminster Abbey has been the coronation church for British monarchs since 1066. Two lofty London plane trees stand guard beside the central path that bisects the expanse of neatly mown lawn – these venerable trees are the oldest in the garden, having been planted in the 1850s. Other trees worth seeking out are the lovely old fig at the far end of the garden (sadly its fruits, although copious, are not worth scrumping), a white mulberry and a 'Kanzan' cherry.

The Little Cloister

En route to the garden (which is accessed via an entrance in Dean's Yard), you will pass two other gardens original to the monastery. The first is The Great Cloister Garth, a dazzlingly minimalist square of immaculately striped lawn where the monk's could recharge their batteries – green being the symbolic colour of rebirth. A little further along is the Little Cloister, a perfectly formed courtyard garden which once served as the Infirmary Garden. This was a therapeutic garden, designed to aid recuperation after illness. It could easily serve this purpose today with its restful colour scheme of silver leafed plants and evergreen topiary and the soothing sound of the water playing in its central fountain.

Westminster College Garden
Westminster Abbey
www.westminster-abbey.org
Tues, Wed, Thurs throughout the year:
Winter 10.00-16.00
Summer: 10.00-18.00

W   What Will the Harvest Be?

Gardens can flourish in unexpected places and this community 'harvest' garden is no exception. Slap bang next to the recently opened Abbey Road DLR station in West Ham, and overlooked by modern industrial buildings, the location is hardly bucolic. In this inauspicious environment the garden was established in the summer of 2009 and has gone on to answer the question it poses with abundant yields of cut flowers, fruit and veg.

Before its makeover the site was a magnet for fly-tippers but its origins are more romantic as it was once part of the 12th-century Abbey of St Mary, Stratford Langthorne. Its current good looks are down to the Friends of Abbey Gardens, who successfully lobbied Newham Council to improve the site. The community garden design is the work of commissioned artists Nina Pope (see her garden on p.306) and Karen Guthrie. Contaminated soil presented an immediate problem but safe growing conditions were created by placing raised beds on top of a 20cm layer of soil buffered by a water permeable membrane. The 34 narrow oak and steel beds, arranged in flag-like strips, were themselves filled with top soil, and in 2009 volunteers set about raising hundreds of seedlings to plant in them.

With its jazzy contemporary styling and emphasis on organic food production and community

involvement, *What will the Harvest Be?* is very much a 21st century creation. But, contemporary as it is, the garden's design and ethos are also steeped in the area's history, with Karen and Nina drawing particular inspiration from the Plaistow Landgrabbers of the early 20th century. The Landgrabbers were a group of unemployed men who in 1906 squatted a disused patch of land in Plaistow, to grow vegetables and show that the unemployed were willing to work. Although their defiant stand against authority was doomed, the Landgrabbers are honoured in Abbey Gardens, where the triangular arrangement of the raised vegetable beds recalls their ill-fated 'Triangle Camp'. The scheme's name derives from a slogan daubed by the Landgrabbers on the wall of their camp.

What will the Harvest be? is run on egalitarian lines, as a shared resource with no one plot being 'owned' or ' managed' by an individual. The garden is open daily and the Friends of Abbey Gardens run free gardening sessions three times a week between March and October. The produce is shared among regular gardeners and the surplus sold via an honesty stall at the garden gate.

What will the Harvest Be?
Abbey Gardens, Opposite Bakers Row, E15 3NF
www.whatwilltheharvestbe.com
www.abbeygardens.org

Wildflower Meadows

There may not have been a cure for the summertime blues in Eddie Cochran's day but in 21st-century London the sight of a wildflower meadow in full bloom certainly lifts the spirits. It's a prospect that's becoming more common too, as local authorities are increasing realizing the environmental and community benefits of urban meadows.

The wildflower meadow that runs alongside the A12, by Mabley Green, was planted by community volunteers, working in partnership with Hackney Council, in response to concerns about a decline in local wildlife. In March 2010, after turf on the green had been stripped back, a 'pictorial meadow' seed mix was scattered and by June it was a blooming carpet of annual cornflowers, poppies, fairy toadflax, bishop's flower and red flax. Since its first season, spring bulbs, perennial wildflowers and grasses have been added to the planting scheme, bringing it more in line with 'traditional' meadows.

Over in west London, the busy A4 has also acquired a wayside wildflower patch. The Hogarth Roundabout Meadow was the brainchild of landscape architect Brita von Schoenaich, who finally got Tranport for London (who manage the site) on board in 2011, after two previous attempts to guerrilla garden the site ended in failure. Third time lucky, TfL rotivated the site for free, while the Old Chiswick Preservation Society sponsored the work. A vibrant mix of native and non-native annuals lights up the meadow through the summer months, providing a source of forage for wildlife and a visual feast for passersby.

www.mableymeadow.blogspot.co.uk
www.schoenaich.co.uk

A wildlife garden in the congested centre of London might sound a quixotic enterprise but since its opening in 1995 the Wildlife Garden at the Natural History Museum has flourished. What was formerly the museum's unprepossessing west garden has been transformed into an evocation of 9 semi-natural habitats, typical of Southern England.

The initial installation in 1994 involved a planting list of some 950 trees and 3800 shrubs, not to mention quantities of herbaceous plants – a seemingly enormous specification for a 1-acre site. But the saturation tactic has paid off, more than 15 years down the line and most of the habitats are successfully established, pulsating with wildlife and feeling surprisingly plausible, despite the proximity of the Cromwell Road.

A gently meandering path leads visitors on a mini safari through fen and reedbed to hedgerow, heathland and woodland. The 'urban wasteland' habitat might seem a bit artificial, but the tough-as-old-boots buddleia, thistles and brambles all have a role to play in nurturing inner city invertebrates – buddleia, an introduction from China, is irresistible to our native butterflies and moths. The chalk downland is more picturesque, a free drawing mound studded with classic downland plants like common toadflax, quaking grass, thyme, oxeye daisies, yarrow and cucumber scented salad burnet. The garden has even attracted the six-belted clearwing moth, *Bembecia ichneumoniformis*, a rare sighting in central London.

The meadow is one of the most satisfying habitats. It is a tiny souvenir of England's agricultural past, luxuriant with grasses (and grasshoppers), clover and cranesbill, common sorrel, meadow vetchling and burdock. The summer flowers are much enjoyed by bees, butterflies and moths. Orchids – common spotted and pyramidal – feature in both the chalk downland and meadow habitats.

Once the meadow flowers have set seed (usually by the end of August), a small flock of grey-faced Dartmoor sheep are bought in to graze in traditional fashion – a popular, if surreal, garden attraction.

The garden's watery habitats are wildlife rich as well, although residents such as water fleas are thankfully invisible to the naked eye. More exciting for most visitors are the bejewelled damsel and dragonflies that flit above the ponds in the summer, and the newts, frogs, moorhens and mallards with whom they share the water. Nature being red in tooth and claw, this abundance of aquatic protein attracts the occasional attention of a visiting grey heron. Thanks to the efforts of volunteers however, the moorhens at least have their own offshore nesting box on an island in the main pond to protect them from the garden's resident foxes.

In spring the woodland habitat is carpeted with wood anemones, bluebells and fragrant wild garlic – through which scuttle mice, toads, spiders, several varieties of woodlice and numerous beetle species including the gloriously named 'Devil's Coach Horse'. Generously planted with native trees such as sessile and pedunculate oak, beech and hawthorn, the garden supports several bee colonies, including one housed in a bespoke 'bee tree', with their honey being harvested in September. The cover provided by the trees and hedgerow makes the garden an attractive proposition for city birds such as blackbirds, blue and long-tailed tits, greenfinches, robins, and Eurasian jays. Other airborne visitors include well over 400 species of butterflies and moths as well as nocturnal visitors such as pipistrelle bats and moths such as the elephant hawkmoth.

An amazing creation, this 'wild' garden is a deceptive one, for its *rus in urbe* idyll is in fact very carefully maintained. Dr Caroline Ware is the wildlife gardener/ecologist who manages the garden, and under her supervision slow to rot plane leaves are raked up, woodland coppiced, unsuitable plant species removed, blanket weed in the pond cleared away, and fragile eco systems balanced. And all the while the garden is monitored by NHM scientists and

a team of volunteers, who keep tabs on everything from algae and lichens upwards. A 'recent sightings' board keeps visitors up to date with what wildlife has been spotted, while strategically placed wooden doors reveal what's going on beneath the topsoil of habitats such as the heathland, or what the bees are up to in their tree.

The garden is open 1 April to 31 October and during this time is well-used by schools and other groups for an ever evolving programme of events, including the always popular activity of pond dipping. A proud Green Flag Award winner, the garden is an inspirational example of how valuable our gardens are to wildlife as well as being a magical place for stressed out urban *homo sapiens*. Additionally, the garden opens for the Yellow Book scheme and the annual London Open Garden Square weekend. See their website for details of events.

The Wildlife Garden
Natural History Museum,
Cromwell Road, SW3
www.nhm.ac.uk

W Wildlife Gardening

The concrete jungle might seem a hostile environment for wildlife but, given a helping hand, wild plants and creatures of all kinds can thrive in the urban landscape. Public wildlife gardens like that at the Natural History Museum (see p.236) and at the Centre for Wildlife Gardening in Peckham (see p.48) are inspirational templates showing how wildlife can be encouraged into the city and the benefits of doing so. On a domestic scale there are plenty of ways to make our own gardens more wildlife friendly, in the process helping to boost local biodiversity and combat the effects of climate change. And with over 3 million gardens in the capital, London's gardeners are well placed to make a significant contribution. Wildlife friendly gardens help to absorb carbon in the atmosphere, offer food and habitat to wildlife and create green wildlife corridors across the city.

Organic

Whatever the size of your plot, be it capacious back garden, standard 10 rod allotment or tiny balcony, going organic is probably the best starting point for the fledgling wildlife gardener. Natural, non-chemical gardening is beneficial for wildlife and humans alike – for example, hand weeding may seem like a chore but it's usually more effective than chemical weed-killers and is great exercise too. Londoners may not have easy access to the horticultural 'black gold' that is horse manure, but it's easy and economical to make your own fertilizers – comfrey or nettle leaves left to rot down in water transform into a foul smelling but effective liquid manure or can be used to activate a compost heap. Organic gardening encourages natural predators, obviating the need for chemical pesticides; frogs and toads help to reduce slug and snail populations, ladybird and lacewing larvae tuck into aphids and garden birds also helpful in controlling insect pests. For really persistent slug problems, microscopic nematodes can be used (available from green gardening suppliers).

Sustainable

An approach to gardening and life in general which aims to have a positive impact on the environment, minimising the unsustainable use of resources. Gardeners can do their bit too:

- avoid buying peat based composts (peat is a non-renewable resource & peat bogs are now one of the UK's most threatened habitats).
- Make your own compost.
- Avoid buying garden furniture made from unsustainably managed tropical hardwoods.
- Harvest your own rain water.
- Recycle and re-use wherever possible – for example return plastic plant pots to point of sale so they can be re-used; broken terracotta pots can be used to improve drainage in other containers.

Gardening for climate change

Flash floods, rising temperatures and drier summers are some of the expected outcomes of climate change in London. Whatever your stance on the climate change debate, there's no denying that this country has experienced some extreme weather events in recent years. Gardeners need to adapt to the changing reality and have an important role to play in reducing London's carbon footprint. Here are a few ideas:

- Plant drought resistant plants.
- Mulch in the spring to conserve moisture levels in the soil.
- Minimize water use – don't mow the lawn so often, water in the evening or early morning and only where needed.
- Harvest rain water & reuse grey water from your bath or shower.
- Extend the green area of your garden by adding a green roof to your shed.
- Don't pave over your front garden – it increases the risk of flooding and displaces wildlife.
- If you have room, plant a broad-leaved native tree or mixed hedge.

Resources

www.britishbee.org.uk

www.bumblebeeconservation.org.uk

www.lbka.org.uk

www.wildlondon.org.uk

www.rhs.org.uk

www.naturalengland.org.uk

www.rspb.org.uk/wildlife/wildlifegarden

www.gardenersworld.com

www.butterfly-conservation.org

Wildlife Garden National
History Museum, see p.236

Attracting Wildlife

Biodiversity is on the decline worldwide but Londoners can become their own conservationists by adopting a wildlife friendly approach to gardening. Attracting wildlife into the garden helps sustain animals threatened by climate change whilst adding interest and vitality to the urban landscape. The London Wildlife Trust (*www.wildlondon.org.uk*) runs a 'Garden for a Living London' campaign and their 'how to' guides are packed with wildlife friendly gardening advice. The RHS (*www.rhs.org.uk*) is also a fertile source of wildlife gardening tips.

In the meantime here are few simple ideas for wildlife friendly gardening:

- Build a pond – it doesn't have to be big and fancy, it could just be an old basin sunk into the lawn. Use native aquatic and marginal plants and don't forget to build up one end so hedgehogs can exit safely.
- Install insect hotels and bird boxes.
- Don't be too tidy – leave areas of long grass for insects and woodpiles for stag beetles.
- Consider the needs of wildlife when maintaining your garden.

Insect hotel

Long grass

Beetle

Pond and bird box

Woodpile

Insect hotel

Plant a butterfly border

Keep your butterflies in nectar from spring through to autumn with a choice selection of tasty flowers. In spring wallflowers and hyacinths could be on the menu while summer butterfly magnets include buddleia, phlox and lavender with Michaelmas daisies, honeysuckle and verbena providing the autumnal rearguard. If you want to provide food for yourself at the same time you could try runner beans, brambles, oregano, chives and raspberries. Make sure your border is south facing and sheltered from the wind and, if you can bear it, try to include some nettles – this much maligned plant supports over 40 insect species and is the larval food plant of choice for red admiral, small tortoiseshell and peacock butterflies. If the thought of actively cultivating nettles in your garden dismays you, plant them in containers and remember that young nettles can be put to culinary use as well as making excellent garden manure. See *www.nettles.org.uk* for more pro-nettle propaganda.

London Butterflies

Two butterflies make reference to London in their names; the Wall Brown butterfly was known as the 'London Eye' in the 18th century and today can occasionally be glimpsed in north London gardens. The rather more flamboyant Camberwell Beauty is a rare migrant to these shores, its first recorded appearance being in Coldharbour Lane in 1748. There are only a few sightings of the elusive Beauty every year, but during 2010's 'Big Butterfly Count' one was spotted not far from London – in Cobham, Surrey.

Camberwell Beauty

Verbena

Wall Brown

Butterfly friendly garden at Hampton Court Flower Show

Bee friendly

Where would we be without the bee? It has been estimated that bees are responsible for 1 in every 3 mouthfuls of the world's food but bee populations are in serious decline. England's bees are vanishing faster than anywhere else in Europe, with loss of habitat, varroa mite and colony collapse disorder among the problems they face. The situation is so bad that the government launched a £10 million project to investigate. In the mean time, gardeners can offer practical help by making their gardens bee friendly and enhancing bee habitats.

Aim to provide visiting bees with nectar from March to September with a succession of easy to access single flowered blooms – think traditional cottage gardens flowers like aquilegias, foxgloves, penstemons, sedum and snapdragons, as well as native wildflowers. Site your bee border in the sun, out of the way of cold winds and plant in drifts to help bees navigate. Opt for flowers in the blue, purple, pink, yellow and white ranges of the colour spectrum and don't forget to put out some water – it's thirsty work foraging for nectar!

The yellow blooms of insect friendly Achillea

A seasonal nectar menu

STARTERS (SPRING):
Daffodil
Bluebell
Crab apple

MAINS (SUMMER):
Aquilegia
Stachys
Delphinium
Dog rose

DESSERTS (LATE SUMMER/ EARLY AUTUMN):
Aster
Lavender
Scabious
Sunflower

A nectar menu to share:
The flowers of many culinary herbs and plants are also very attractive to bee so it's possible to create a bee border that is also edible: Broad Bean, Rosemary, Fennel, Thyme, Chives, Angelica, Borage, Pot marigold, Globe artichoke.

Field Scabious

Rosa rugosa

Sunflower

Runner Bean

Globe Artichoke

Dahlia

insect hotel

Insects are an integral part of natural eco-systems and in a garden context they are vital because they eat pests and pollinate plants and in turn provide food for birds and other wildlife. Beneficial insects such as ladybirds can be encouraged into the garden through wildlife friendly management techniques (see p.243), and by making 'hotels' which they can check into over the winter months to hibernate and lay eggs.

When it comes to setting yourself up as an insect hotelier, no great technical prowess is required. Small-scale boutique bug hotels can be made by drilling holes in a block of wood or tying together a bundle of hollow bamboo canes; block up one end to exclude draughts and hang from a tree or place against a sheltered wall. Wooden pallets, stacked on top of each other, are perfect for larger constructions – just fill the gaps with insect friendly material like straw, dry leaf litter, pine cones, wood chippings or corrugated card. If pallets prove too cumbersome, a similar effect can be achieved by making a layered structure using bricks and wooden boards.

Although there are no planning permits or building regulations to worry about it is worth following a few guidelines:

- Keep the rain out by providing a waterproof roof for your hotel. This doesn't have to be fancy - old roof tiles or a board covered with roofing felt or simple plastic sheeting will do. The waterproof membrane can be covered with gravel and soil and planted with sedum to create a green roofed hostelry with 5 star wildlife credentials.

- Leave plenty of gaps and holes to give your new guests space to move around and make themselves at home.

- Invertebrates, like students, prefer damp shady living quarters so site your stack in moist, dappled shade if possible.

- There's something highly satisfying about building a bug home and then watching your garden fill with new insect life. Your guests might not bother to post a review on TripAdvisor but they will reward you in other ways – devouring garden pests like greenfly, pollinating flowers and fruit trees, and making your garden more bio-diverse.

Trellick Bee Tower, Roots & Shoots, see p.188

Bee tree

A colony of honey bees is using this tree trunk as their home. About 15,000 bees live here. The hive houses more than just bees — there are also eggs, young bees and honey.

Bee busy

The bees work together to find and store food and look after the queen and young bees. The queen is the only bee in the hive who lays eggs.

Honey bees eat nectar, which they find in flowers. They use nectar to make honey. They visit 50–100 flowers in one trip and can find nectar up to five kilometres away. If they discover a good source of nectar they tell the other bees back at the hive by moving in different patterns and shakes called a 'waggle dance'.

Bee helpful

When bees collect nectar from flowers, they also collect pollen. As they fly from plant to plant, they transfer the pollen, helping the plants reproduce. Gardens with lots of different plant species support more wildlife and make a healthier habitat. These bees will pollinate flowers up to five kilometres away, helping to keep this area's flowering plants diverse and healthy.

Don't worry, bee happy

Bees can sting, but only if they feel threatened. If a bee flies up to you, it is trying to find out if you are a food source. The best way to make a bee go away is to stay still and it will fly off.

W Winter at Kew

The Pagoda, Kew

Kew's historic glasshouses are the obvious destination on a cold, wet winter's day, a low carbon way to experience exotic flora without cashing in your Oyster card for a plane ticket.

Rising up out of the earth like an enormous glass submarine, the Palm House is probably Kew's most iconic building. It was built in the mid 1840s to a design by Decimus Burton, to house the palms collected by Victorian plant hunters. Today it's home to *Encephalartos altensteinii*, a venerable palm which has lived through Kew's entire history, having been collected in Africa by Kew's first plant hunter Francis Masson in the early 1770s. Shy and retiring these plants ain't – some of them, like the fishtail palm from Indonesia, soar metres high up to the roof. Carefully placed signs remind visitors to 'look up' to admire the taller specimens. Many plants are reminders of our indebtedness to the plant world – where would we be without the tamarind tree to provide one of the ingredients in Worcester Sauce? More seriously, leukaemia sufferers benefit from the alkaloids found in the sap of the Madagascar periwinkle.

With a cosy minimum year round temperature of 18°C, the Temperate House is a perfect winter destination for non-hardy human visitors. This mighty glass cathedral measures 4,880 metres square, making it the largest surviving Victorian glasshouse in the world – twice the size of its older sibling, the Palm House. Behind its glass walls lies a lush world of tender plants from the world's mountains, oceanic islands and savannahs. The geographical

planting scheme leads the visitor across continents to encounter plants such as *Dicksonia antarctica* (Australia), the multi-talented date palm (Europe), *Tetrapanax papyfer*, the plant used to make edible rice paper (Asia) and life-saving plants such as anti-malarial quinine (America). If the medicines don't work, there's always *Taiwania cryptomerioides* – the coffin tree (Taiwan). This is also the place to discover the disconcerting fact that, like money, bananas don't grow on trees – bananas being herbaceous plants. Following a top-to-toe refurb in the 1980s, growing conditions in the Temperate House are now so optimum that many residents have flowered, some, like the *Protea cynaroides* (king protea), for the first time since the 19th century.

It's one thing to admire exotic plants in the climate controlled comfort of a glasshouse, quite another to study them in their, often unforgiving, native habitats. Marianne North, an indefatigable Victorian traveller was one such pioneer. At the age of 41 – and without any formal artistic training – she embarked on a 13-year painting odyssey, travelling the world with the aim of painting plants in their habitats. An accomplished and prolific artist, by the end of her travels, Marianne had depicted over 900 plant species in 833 paintings. She created a unique record of the plant world which she donated to Kew together with a purpose built gallery – a curious red-brick amalgam of Greek temple and Indian colonial bungalow (complete with verandah). Memorably described by Wilfred Blunt as a 'botanical stamp album', the collection is arranged geographically

with the vividly coloured landscapes covering every square inch of wall space. First opened in 1882, the gallery has recently been restored, with additions of 21st century interpretive displays – making the Marianne North Gallery a must-see on a visit to Kew.

Adjoining the MNG is the Shirley Sherwood Gallery of Botanical Art, a sleek white gallery space that opened in 2008. It's the first gallery in the world to be devoted to botanical art and shows works from Kew's own ever expanding archive of botanical illustrations, and the Shirley Sherwood collection of contemporary botanical art. Exhibitions change thrice yearly, but in a welcome departure from most galleries' practice, there is always work on display even during changeover periods.

Year-round interest is the holy grail for most gardeners and – as you might expect from this centre of horticultural excellence – it's a feat that Kew pulls off in some style. If you're determined to go outside, head for the Winter Garden. Appropriately, Kew's historic ice house lies at the centre of this seasonal garden, planted to give interest in December and January. Scented plants come into their own at this time and visitors to the Winter Garden can breathe in the delicious fragrance of winter flowering plants such as *Sarcococca humilis*, *Mahonia x media* 'Winter Sun' or the chocolate scented *Azara microphylla*. Early spring bulbs add further floriferous appeal – among those braving the cold are anemones, hellebores and crocus. There's no need to limit yourself to the Winter Garden. Swathes of cheerful yellow aconites underpin the Holly Walk – which also looks superb in winter – and pale carpets of snowdrop can be found near the Temple of Aeolus, the Ruined Arch and in the Rock Garden. The conifers and broad leaved evergreen trees of the arboretum look good whatever the weather, and as winter turns to spring, willow catkins enliven proceedings with a promise of good things to come.

Royal Botanic Gardens
Kew, Richmond, Surrey, TW9
www.kew.org
T:020 8332 5655 (visitor information)

Just 25 miles from central London, for out-of-town horticultural gratification, Wisley is hard to beat. As its capacious car and coach parking would suggest, the flagship garden of RHS is something of a shrine, and it attracts nigh on a million green-fingered pilgrims each year.

With 240 acres at its disposal, the garden is enjoyably multi-faceted, allowing visitors to roam around an alpine meadow one minute, and through a tropical rainforest the next. For first timers a free guided tour is a good way to get your bearings and see features you perhaps wouldn't otherwise notice, such as the naturally grafted oak tree by the ornamental entrance gates or the oldest tree in the rock garden, a bonsai larch tree imported from Japan in 1904.

Wisley's legions of repeat visitors appreciate its subtle seasonal variations and its adventurous approach to gardening. Wisley was gifted to the RHS in 1903 as an experimental garden, a tradition which continues to this day, with Wisley's annual trials of fruit, veg and flowers to determine which varieties should receive the coveted Award of Garden Merit. Even the rambling timber and brick Tudor style 'country pile' overlooking the canal and loggia is in fact a laboratory, teeming with soil scientists, plant pathologists and botanists.

While the RHS scientists, staff and students beaver away, visitors can admire the fruit of their labour in the immaculately tended garden. One of the joys of Wisley is seeing things done properly, the 'RHS way'. In the fruit demonstration garden this means a masterclass in precisely pruning and training apples and pears, while the ambitious new Bowes-Lyon rose garden promises a sea of David Austin roses. The Penelope Hobhouse designed Country Garden is an essay in understated English style, while the long mixed borders unfold an epic sweep in high summer. 'Bowles' Corner' commemorates the great horticulturalist E A Bowles, whose name also lives on in many popular garden plants, and whose own garden at Myddelton House has recently been restored (see p.160).

Productive gardening gets plenty of space, with a comprehensive herb garden, vegetable garden, a 16-acre 'fruit field' planted with over 2,000 trees, and a wine-producing vineyard. A cluster of model gardens provides inspirational templates for those wanting to make the most of small gardens. Sometimes described as the 'jewel of Wisley', the alpine display house shines brightly even in the depths of winter with daily changing displays of these tenacious little plants, which may include cyclamen, narcissi, saxifrages and auriculas, according to season. Alpines get an outdoor airing in the newly built 'crevice garden' and in the nearby alpine meadow, with its drifts of crocuses, cyclamen-flowered daffodils and dog's tooth violets. Descending dramatically down the hillside from the alpine department are the cascades and pools of the rock garden, which celebrated its centenary in 2011. If all this alpine activity gets too chilly, the state of the art glasshouse offers warmer territory to explore, and the company of lush tropical and temperate plants, exotic orchids and the odd oversized butterfly.

With its light, acidic soil, Wisley puts on a dazzling late spring show of rhododendrons, azaleas, magnolias and camellias in the winding woodland paths of Battleston Hill and in the Wild Garden. Its ericaceous soil also makes it a natural location for the national heather collection and a pinetum that boasts several Champion trees.

A million visitors a year can't be wrong – Wisley tends its human visitors as carefully as it does its plants, with an appealing mix of eateries, well-stocked shop and plant sales area, a stimulating programme of events and specialist plant shows and probably the world's best garden bookshop. RHS members enjoy the added benefit of free entry and the possibility of personal gardening advice from Wisley's advisors.

RHS Garden Wisley
Woking, Surrey, GU23 6QB
www.rhs.org.uk/wisley
T: 0845 260 9000

W World's End Nurseries

The King's Road has seen more than its fair share of fashion fads over the years, but with nearly four decades of trading under its belt, this Chelsea nursery is something of a timeless classic. Established by James Lotery in 1972, and now managed by James' son Janson, the nursery occupies an enviable one-acre site, making it one of the largest of its kind in central London (although as a retail nursery none of the stock is actually raised on site).

The ivy covered entrance archway with its naively painted sign is something of a local landmark and invites visitors to enter a green and pleasant world. Beyond the arch, the ambience is deceptively rustic – in fact the nursery is very much geared to the needs of the city gardener. With year-round interest at a premium in the concrete jungle, hardworking evergreens, in a variety of guises, are a mainstay here. Elegant bay and box lollipops, spirals and pyramids confer instant formal structure to the city garden but, proving that the London gardener can have his cake and eat it, there are also flowering evergreens such as camellias, ceanothus and rhododendrons to provide seasonal splashes of colour. Olive trees are bestsellers here and there's a good show of lavenders for optimistic Londoners hoping to recreate the south of France closer to home. Indoor gardeners are well served too. Sheltering in the warmth of the glass house are tender orchids, fuzzy leaved African violets, gaudy Guzmanias, spiky cactus and fragrant pelargoniums. The nursery cat snoozing in the warmth, is also a regular feature of the glass house.

It's not just the postcode that's chic, the nursery's clientele is as fashionable as the locale – although Janson is far too discreet to name drop. He and his team are down-to-earth and welcoming and their prices reasonable. As well as selling plants, the nursery can plan, plant and maintain your garden and they offer a free consultation and design service, tackling anything from rock stars' herb gardens to council house balconies. Their experienced gardeners are used to negotiating front door access only gardens (and the acres of cream carpet that inevitably lie in between). For clients who insist on getting their hands dirty, the nursery sells a practical range of plant care materials, from compost to pesticides and fertilisers. Janson's top tip is 'anything can grow in a pot – as long as the pot is the right size' and to this end, he stocks a wide selection of containers, including some handsome imported Italian terracotta pots. There are also quirky bits of garden sculpture, trellising and troughs. His other bit of advice ('don't expect the rain to water your plants') can be heeded by simply purchasing a watering can.

World's End Nurseries
441-457 King's Road, SW10 0LR
www.worldsendnurseries.com
T: 020 7351 3343
Open: Mon-Sat 9.00-18.00; Sun 10.00-17.00

A prize-winning City garden

W Worshipful Company of Gardeners

Today a thoroughly modern institution, the Gardeners' livery company has its origins in the medieval craft guilds, and was incorporated by Royal Charter in 1605. As a 'living guild' it numbers professional and amateur horticulturalists among its membership and its charitable activities focus on promoting the art and practice of good gardening, particularly in the London area.

The most colourful manifestation of the Company's work is the long-running 'Flowers in the City' competition, organised jointly with the Corporation of London. The aim is to beautify the City by encouraging the display of foliage and flowers by the private sector. Prizes are awarded for summer and winter displays with categories including best floral street, atrium, livery hall, and courtyard. The much-coveted plaques are presented to winning displays and adorn window boxes and planters around the City with some perennially successful entrants proudly displaying a swath of awards .

However, the Company has not forsaken its historic past and every year on Whit Tuesday, the Fairchild Lecture (formerly known as the 'Vegetable Sermon') is delivered at St Giles Cripplegate, in accordance of the will of the 18th-century Hoxton nurseryman, Thomas Fairchild. The author of a popular manual

for urban gardens, *The City Gardener* (published in 1722), Fairchild was the first person to create a hybrid plant, a cross between a carnation and a Sweet William that became known as 'Fairchild's Mule'. The God-fearing nurseryman was evidently keen to atone for his presumption at usurping the Creator, since the sermon he endowed either takes as its subject the 'Wonderful Works of God in the Creation,' or the 'Certainty of the Resurrection of the Dead, proved by the certain changes of the animal and vegetable parts of the Creation.'

Incidentally, Thomas Fairchild's grave can be found in Hackney Road recreation ground, not far from Columbia Road market. Sadly neglected in recent times, plans are afoot for its restoration as part of a renovation of the park planned by a newly set up 'Friends of Fairchild's Garden' group.

www.gardenerscompany.org.uk
www.flowersinthecity.org.uk

Top right: Thomas Fairchild's grave marker

X   X-Factor

Simon Cowell eat your heart out – show-biz ain't got nothing on horticulture when it comes to the competitive spirit. From the high-stakes drama of Medals' Day at Chelsea Flower Show (p.50) to nail-biting needle matches at the local horticultural show, London's gardeners are spoilt for choice in their quest for gardening glory.

Perhaps it's the essentially solitary, contemplative aspect of gardening that brings out the desire for its practitioners to prove themselves against their peers. Civic pride is at stake too with competitions such as London in Bloom and Flowers in the City encouraging local communities and businesses to go head-to-head in the struggle for floral excellence. Meanwhile parks and public spaces can compete for one of Keep Britain Tidy's coveted Green Flag Awards, which recognise and reward the best green spaces in the country.

RHS Horticultural Halls

Unsurprisingly, London tends to do rather well at this and in 2011 received a record-breaking 227 Green Flag and Community Awards.

Even kids get a look in, thanks to the twice-yearly competitions that are organised by the London Children's Flower Society. Every year some 30,000 children, from around 200 primary and special needs schools in London, take part – growing bulbs for the spring competition and flowers, vegetables and herbs for the summer one.

Participants are given simple instructions on how to raise the plants, which they nurture at home, or tend in the school garden, before bringing them back to school for judging. Cups, trophies and gardening goodies are awarded to the winners at a special ceremony held at Guildhall in the autumn.

www.londoninbloom.co.uk
www.lcfs.olaves.net
www.greenflag.keepbritaintidy.org
www.conservationfoundation.co.uk

The Yellow Book

Visiting other people's gardens is a long-standing British pastime (just read Jane Austen) and it's one that the National Gardens Scheme has harnessed to charitable effect. Their annually produced *Yellow Book* (named after its signature cover colour) is the Bible of committed garden visitors. It is a county-by-county cornucopia of the 3,600, mostly private, gardens in England and Wales that throw their gates open to the public for the scheme every year.

Although entrance fees are kept low (for years it was just 'a shilling a head'), since its foundation in 1927, the NGS has raised over £42 million for selected cancer, nursing and gardening charities.

Powered by a small paid staff and an army of volunteers the NGS has become a much-loved institution. In London it is something of a growth industry, with visitors jumping at the chance to explore some of the capital's most remarkable private gardens. London County Organiser (and current NGS Chairman) Penny Snell has seen the number of open gardens in London climb from just 31 when she started in 1980 to a whopping 250 in 2011, attracting an annual audience of around 18,000 visitors and raising over £145,000. Recently there's also been a gratifying widening in the NGS demographic, and what used to be a rather middle-aged pursuit, today attracts younger visitors as well as more youthful garden owners – a reflection of current enthusiasm for the joys of gardening.

Every year Penny and her treasured team of volunteers search out suitable new gardens to open in the capital. They are often acting on tip-offs from neighbours or contacted direct by owners, keen to share their gardens with others. Always looking to raise standards, Penny's selection criteria are stringent with prospective gardens having to show strong design and horticultural interest as well being immaculately maintained. Practicalities such as parking have to be considered and an extrovert owner is a plus, since they will be bombarded with questions from inquisitive visitors. A long season of interest is another holy grail for the organisers, to avoid a glut of rose-filled June gardens.

Penny's decades of hard work mean that Londoners are truly spoiled with the range of gardens they can find in *The Yellow Book*. From newly minted designer plots to well-established walled gardens; from blowsy Arts and Crafts cottage borders to über-urban roof-terraces and floating barge gardens – they're all here. There are gardens with different soil types and every conceivable aspect and scale from woodland glades to south-facing suntraps, from pocket-handkerchief patios to jam-packed plantsmen's playgrounds. Recent years have seen the increasing appearance of fruit and veg in otherwise decorative private gardens and, adding further to the variety, public-spirited community gardens and allotments now open for the scheme.

Great fun to visit – and often with the added attractions of delicious home-made teas, plant sales and invigorating horticultural chat – open gardens are a brilliant resource. The event shows what can be achieved in real gardens, from clever ideas for the classic rectangular London back garden to tips on making the most of minimal spaces. Group openings are a particularly appealing feature of the NGS in London, much prized for their friendly, festive ambience, and ideal for visitors wishing to see several gardens in one hit. Having given away over £25 million to good causes in the past 15 years, the NGS proves that charity really can begin at home – or at least in the garden.

www.ngs.org.uk

Molly St Hilaire's garden

The Reverend Kemmyo Taira Sato

Z Zen Garden

When it comes to Zen gardens, less is more. This one, behind the suburban villa that houses the Three Wheels Buddhist Centre, is no exception. Although the garden's pared down design is the work of an Englishman, art history professor John White, it has all the elements of an authentic Kyoto Zen garden. Typical features include a carefully considered arrangement of rocks and mosses, meticulously raked gravel, surrounding cob wall, tree-lined perimeter and the thatched meditation hut.

The garden was built from scratch in 1996, a year after the house had been acquired for the Three Wheels Centre as the London outpost of the Shogyoji Temple in Japan. Taking the theme of 'Harmony within Diversity' as its guiding principle, the garden's spiritual purpose came into play even during its construction. Deliberately eschewing mechanical aides, the site was cleared entirely by hand by volunteers from Japan, Britain and elsewhere, who as they worked together were able to gain a deeper understanding of each other, and each other's culture.

Meanwhile, Professor White and the priest at Three Wheels, Reverend Kemmyo Taira Sato, had already set out on a series of journeys to Cumbria to handpick 8 of the 12 rocks that form the backbone of the garden's layout. The remaining four came, rather more prosaically, from a specialist company in Drayton. The 12 rocks resonate with meanings, both visible and otherwise, and in keeping with Zen tradition some are deeply embedded, so that only the smallest proportion of the rock can be seen above ground. Their number recalls the 12 chromatic tones of *Gagaku,* an ancient form of classical Japanese music, the Apostles and the 12 types of light that Amida Buddha radiates. Professor White's arrangement of the rocks invokes the system underlying the Fibonacci sequence.

Designed as an aid to meditation, this is a garden for looking at, not walking through. Its immaculate gravel 'sea' is raked and weeded every two weeks by a trained assistant, using specialist tools (a job that takes up to 5 hours). The L-shaped thatched meditation hut is raised to allow the garden to be seen clearly. Planting is restricted to the trees that run in a metre wide strip behind the cob wall; these pines, laurels, hollies, maples, weeping birch and magnolia represent the *shakkei*, or surrounding scenery. Over time the trees have grown and obscured the garden's actual, urban location; likewise the rocks have taken on a life of their own and, colonised by native mosses and water marks, they have become like mini mountain islands, anchored in their sea of gravel. With nothing to do but absorb the garden's tranquility, visitors experience this garden in a very different way to the average English plot, as suggested by Professor White's poem, written to be read while viewing the garden (see the following page).

The garden is open to the public on selected days through the NGS.

Three Wheels Buddhist Centre
55 Carbery Avenue, Acton, W3 9AB
www.threewheels.org.uk
www.ngs.org.uk

You can make of the garden
what you will.

But it may, perhaps,
make something of you,
which you were not,

if you wait and are still;

if you become one
with the garden
and move beyond thought
or imagination,

and are,
as the garden,
is.

The Chase, Clapham, see 'The Plantsman', p.308

MEET THE
GARDENERS

A Garden Reborn

Taking on someone else's award-winning garden might seem a little daunting but that's exactly the prospect that Ben Nel and Darren Henderson faced when they bought their basement flat in Hackney.

The previous owner had been an enthusiastic actor-cum-gardener who drew on his theatrical background to create a much-fêted garden, which opened for the NGS every year. And just to make life really interesting for the fledgling horticulturalists, their new garden embraced two completely different styles, a formal Italian garden near the house and, at the far end of the garden, a small but fully-fledged Japanese stroll garden, complete with meandering stream, red lacquered 'Shinkyo' bridge and tea house. Inexperienced as they were, Ben and Darren threw themselves into the challenge and within months were being invited to re-open the garden for the NGS.

Unlike most new home owners, Ben and Darren gave priority to the garden over their flat. They lost no time in seeking help about how to care for their unusual and beautiful acquisition. Gardening books were bought and pored over, helpful neighbours (who had watched the garden's evolution over the years) offered advice, and they hired a specialist Japanese gardener to teach them the pruning methods required to keep the box and yew in perfect shape.

Since a lot of specimens in the Japanese garden – their favourite area – had died, some expensive trips to specialist Japanese garden centres were required to hunt down suitable replacement dwarf pines, water lilies, ferns and grasses. But the effort was worth it – in the process Ben and Darren came to understand how the miniature landscapes of a Japanese garden should function to create peace and harmony, and they were

determined to find the right plants for it, instead of simply impulse buying at the local garden store – 'so easy to get carried away!'

Replacement plants were also needed to fill the dozens of characterful old terracotta pots that furnish the Italian garden. Ben and Darren chose a white colour scheme to stand out against this area's stately cypress trees and evergreen box and yew topiary and ordered hundreds of lilies, hyacinths and tulips from Crocus for a radiant spring display. John Innes 2 & 3 was found to be the perfect growing medium for the pots but Darren quickly learned to cut in chicken wire to stop the grey squirrels from stealing the bulbs.

Although respectful of the garden they inherited, they are gradually introducing new features, such as Ben's bamboo edging along the freshly laid blue chipped slate path, inspired by the Kyoto Garden in Holland Park (see p.138). They have also created a new secret dining space under the cloud-like canopy of the ceanothus and have even found time to turn their attentions to the front garden. Ben and Darren are learning all the time but, inspired by positive feedback they got from their NGS visitors, they are determined to carry on developing the garden and make it even more their own.

Navarino Road, Hackney, E8
www.ngs.org.uk
www.crocus.co.uk

A Wildlife Garden

The construction of a studio in the garden a couple of years ago was the impetus for artists Andrew and Karen to redesign the remaining space with fauna-friendliness as its main focus. Combining an informal, slightly Japanese aesthetic with robust, mainly native shrubs and perennials, the garden is gratifyingly low-maintenance, requiring just a couple of annual weeding sessions.

It's not every gardener who will enthusiastically point out a dock or a nettle, but such 'weeds' are welcomed here, with the nettle's traditional counterpart, the dock being prized as much for its autumn colour as its utility as the favoured food of many moth species. Bees meanwhile flock to the green alkanet (*Pentaglottis sempervivens*), comfrey (*Symphytum officinale),* Jacob's Ladder (*Polemonium caeruleum*), and ornamental thistle (*Cirsium rivulare)* that spill onto the path that winds along to the studio. Mediterranean plants such as oleander, olive and lavender also play their part in this buzzing glade, in which Andrew & Karen often see at least 4 or 5 different bee species at any time. Despite suffering the odd visitation of lavender beetle, the couple recommend lavender as a great plant for London as it does so well on the city's dry conditions. They source their plants from their local garden centre, Growing Concerns.

The nature pond is the engine room of the garden's mini eco-system, and plays host to frogs, waterboatmen, damselflies and hoverflies, confirming Andrew's belief that 'water is the best thing to have in your garden in London'. Hand-dug by Andrew to a depth of 4 feet to ensure that it doesn't silt up too quickly, it is slightly raised so it can be seen and enjoyed from the house. Watery landscapes such as Rainham Marshes and Wicken Fen are two of the inspirations behind the

Ornamental thistle and Green alkanet

naturalism of Karen and Andrew's garden,
with nearby city farms and the wildflower
meadows in Mile End Park providing ideas
closer to home.

Rainham Marshes
Purfleet, Essex, RM19 1SZ
www.rsbp.org.uk
T: 01708 899840

Growing Concerns
2 Wick Lane, London E3 2NA
www.growingconcerns.org
T: 020 8985 3222

"I have very little concept of what's a weed, and what's not a weed."

"My gardening adventures have opened my eyes to a new side of London, and the project has been the force behind new friendships."

Adventures on a Rooftop

An unprepossessing 3 metre square flat roof has proved fertile ground for writer and journalist Helen Babbs, providing her with a blank canvas for an experimental edible aerial garden. It has also proved the launch-pad for an acclaimed blog and book about her rooftop gardening odyssey.

An interest in urban ecology and a fascination with London's wildlife provided the initial spur behind both garden and blog. Gardening organically and with an eye to encouraging wildlife, Helen grows masses of flowers to attract bees and moths, and the rooftop also receives frequent visits from chirpy Cockney sparrows and blackbirds. Destructive snails and squirrels also swing by from time to time, but any horticultural setbacks are outweighed by the pleasure of spying a great spotted woodpecker or bats from Helen's rooftop eyrie.

Most gardeners are obsessed by seasonal interest but, as befits the size of her plot, Helen's approach is even more focused. Hers is a rooftop designed for nocturnal as well as diurnal pleasure, where Helen can snooze in the sun or moon-bathe surrounded by plants such as tobacco and evening primrose, which impart their delicious fragrance under cover of darkness.

Sandwiched between the Camden and Holloway Roads, the roof garden is a surprisingly tranquil domain, although the neighbourhood's dawn chorus (which Helen has recorded for her blog) gives the Holloway traffic a run for its money. Keeping to a strictly peat-free planting regime, Helen has successfully raised potatoes, beans, tomatoes, courgettes, garlic, strawberries and herbs on her postage-stamp patch, and entertained friends

with zero-food mile dinner parties. Although, by Helen's own admission, the rooftop has evolved haphazardly, its guiding principles are that it should be low maintenance and low cost. With this in mind, street finds such as a discarded wicker picnic basket are adopted to provide the savvy author with both a budget planter and the material for a post…

My Garden, the City and Me – Rooftop Adventures in the Wilds of London, Timber Press

www.aerialediblegardening.co.uk

An Architect's Garden

Visitors to Deborah Nagan's and Michael Johnson's garden enjoy two for the price of one. The front garden, just off the busy Brixton Road, is a formerly neglected space that has been transformed into a productive patch, kitted out with raised vegetable beds and colourful, outsized bean pole wigwams. To the rear of the house a double-height glass extension was the springboard for a lawn-free garden arranged over two tiers, consisting of a basement garden with pond and an upper level with more raised beds, grey slate paddlestone paving, and abundantly planted with a focus on perennial flowers and fruit trees.

Respectively a landscape architect and an architect, Deborah and Michael divide their work in the garden, with Deborah looking after the soft landscaping, Michael the hard. The result of all this design know-how is that house and garden work together cohesively, with clever details (a stone floor that flows 'through' the glass wall from the garden into the house) and imaginative materials (a fence fashioned from salvaged floorboards, rusted metal raised beds). As well as blurring the usual boundaries between house and garden, the glass extension reflects light back into the garden – so much so that the flowers turn their faces to it in preference to the sun.

Although a self-confessed minimalist, Deborah has created her own garden along more fulsome lines, choosing plants that are 'a bit rampant' so she can chop them down to make compost. Bought-in compost replaced the garden's original poor soil but over the years Deborah has added her own home produced compost. The garden is now abundantly fertile with empire-building clumps of over-wintered dahlias and bumper crops of raspberries and

"...the glass extension reflects light back into the garden – so much so that the flowers turn their faces to it in preference to the sun."

blackberries. Fruits that aren't eaten straight off the cane are turned into jam and even the berries on the *Sambucus nigra* 'Black Lace' are eyed up for their culinary potential. Conditions are less favourable in the front garden, which is both windy and shaded by a thirsty horse chestnut tree. An organic gardener 'by default', Deborah gets around the slug/snail problem by simply avoiding plants that they like and finds cats, with their unerring talent for sitting on newly planted specimens, more of a pest.

The handsome tree fern that stands sentinel by the pond thrives on neglect; it was placed here early in the garden's genesis but serendipitously looks fantastic viewed from above. More considered is the garden's year-round interest, which embraces the keenly anticipated witch hazel flowers in February, the pristine lily of the valley in May and the glowing autumnal hues of Virginia creeper and ornamental vine. The garden has a rusty colour scheme, with a painterly palette of wine-dark dahlias, magenta penstemons, pink sedum and rose campion and dusky *Ophiopogon nigrescens*. The space recalls one of Deborah's favourite London places, the Rothko Room at Tate Modern, of which she says, 'I don't see much difference between that and a garden – it seems to me to be a bit of a garden.'

Brixton Road, SW9
www.ngs.org.uk
www.naganjohnson.co.uk

An Easy Maintenance Garden

All too often conjuring visions of soulless gravel and excessive hard-landscaping, the beautiful, horticulturally interesting, low-maintenance garden is a hard trick to pull off. Paul & Janet Barry's garden in Dulwich shows the doubters how it's done.

Having lived with the rather dated garden they inherited when they moved in 25 years ago, the couple commissioned Ian Smith and Debbie Roberts of Acreswild to redesign the garden back in 2006/7.

As well as being easy to care for, Paul and Janet also wanted the garden to have a slightly tropical feel with lots of foliage and scent, and to be a peaceful, secluded space. The result is a sensuous urban sanctuary, which features a delightful interplay of texture and colour between plants such as *Dicksonia antarctica* (Australian tree fern) and *Fargesia nitida* (bamboo), and glaucous-leaved hostas alongside purple leaved phormiums and the golden grass *Hakonechloa macra* 'Aureola' (grass). Flowers haven't been entirely forsaken for foliage, with day lilies, hellebores and geraniums punctuating the greenery; while fragrant *Clematis armandii*, honeysuckle and jasmine keep the garden supplied with the scent that Janet loves.

Unusually for a low maintenance design, the garden includes a lawn and a pond. While Janet enjoys mowing the former ('it immediately makes the garden look nice'), a local contractor takes care of seasonal tasks such as weeding, feeding and scarification. The pond, with its waterlilies and marginal plantings of arum lilies and *Carex elata* 'aurea', may demand a bit of attention (it's prone to blanket weed) but the extra labour is forgiven in view of its central role in the garden's design and its success in attracting wildlife, such as birds, frogs and bees.

Easily maintained on a regime of gentle, 'therapeutic' pottering and twice-yearly pruning sessions to keep plants the right size, Janet and Paul's garden is a revelation for anyone who feels they are a slave to horticulture. Opening for the NGS admittedly adds an extra element of commitment to the enterprise, but both Paul and Janet appreciate the discipline of having a deadline to work to – and the glowing feedback from visitors.

Half-Moon Lane, SE24
www.ngs.co.uk
www.acreswild.co.uk

"I really love the smell of honeysuckle."

287

PLANTLIST:

TREES
Acer ginnala (Amur maple)
Acer palmatum 'Dissectum'
(Japanese maple)
Acer palmatum 'Senkaki'

CLIMBERS
Clematis armandii

SHRUBS
Buxus sempervirens (box)
Callistemon subulatus (bottlebrush)
Viburnum x bodnantense 'Dawn'

BAMBOOS, FERNS & GRASSES
Carex elata 'Aurea'
(Bowles' golden sedge)
Dicksonia antartica
(Australian tree fern)
Dryopteris erythrosora (fern)
Fargesia murieliae 'Simba'
(bamboo)
Fargesia nitida (bamboo)
Hakonechloa macra 'Aureola'
Matteuccia struthiopteris
(shuttlecock fern)
Miscanthus floridulus
Miscanthus sinensis 'Ferner Osten'
Miscanthus sinensis 'Malepartus'

HERBACEOUS & BULBS
Erigeron karvinskianus (fleabane)
Euphorbia mellifera (honey spurge)
Geranium 'Johnson's Blue'
Geranium macrorrhizum 'Album'
Geranium renardii
Helleborus foetidus (hellebore)
Hemerocallis 'Eenie Fanfare' (dwarf
daylily)

POND PLANTS
Butomus umbellatus
(flowering rush)
Iris laevigata (Japanese water iris)

David's Ecohouse

A former car-breaker's yard might not appear the most propitious site for a house, or a garden for that matter. It is on just such unforgiving terrain that David Matzdorf has built his eco-friendly house and created not one but two distinct gardens: an experimental green roof and a 'modern exotic' terrestrial front garden.

Accessible only by ladder, the roof is where David pushes the boundaries of accepted green roof wisdom. Here the usual ground-hugging sedums are joined by loftier, more adventurous plant choices such as spiky dasylirion from Mexico and fascicularia, a Chilean bromeliad whose spiny foliage turns crimson in the autumn. Brightly flowered drought resistant plants such as cistus, thrift (*Armeria maritima*), mesembryanthemum and aromatic chives ensure this roofscape doesn't turn brown, as 'green' roofs have a tendency to do. Cranesbills also do well up here and David particularly recommends *Geranium x oxonianum* 'Wargrave Pink' as a resilient London plant.

David's gently sloping 'horticultural green roof' has evolved since the house was completed in 2000. The 90:10 topsoil/sharp sand mix that was delivered in place of the 60:40 mix originally ordered has caused a few headaches along the way, not least in its hospitality to perennial weeds. But in deciding to 'rise above' the weed problem by planting taller plants David has discovered that it is possible to grow a wider range of plants – particularly succulents and xerophytic shrubs – than is usually thought possible in London. Ever experimental, he uses lightweight perlite to make mounds to raise the height of certain specimens and increase the standard 100mm soil depth.

Mesembryanthemum

Thrift (Armeria maritima)

While the roof garden resembles alpine scree, down at ground level it's a different story. Tucked between house and boundary wall, the microclimate here is tropical with planting to match. With the glass façade of the house looking directly onto the garden, David has opted for evergreen, architectural plants to give him year-round interest. The garden is a lushly textured palette of cordyline, bamboo, yucca, banana, acacia, abutilon and David's cosseted brugmansias. The latter are overwintered inside but other plants have to take their chances outdoors. Against expectation the *Phoenix canariensis* (date palm) has grown into a 6m wide by 4.5m high giant, requiring a once sunny area to become a shady home for rodgersias and ferns. With fathomless London clay to contend with there was no option but to import topsoil; the plants in the lower garden flourish in a 500-600mm layer of clayey loam, laid over a mulch of rotted organic material.

A plantsman to his fingertips, David shuns expensive hard landscaping in favour of plants, plants and yet more plants – most of them propagated at home or acquired through plant swaps. As a living experiment, the garden is in an ongoing state of flux and suburban tidiness is not on the agenda. What David most enjoys about gardening is 'Changing things. Then watching them change themselves. Gardens are never finished.' The garden opens for the NGS and by appointment between May and October.

Hungerford Road, N7
www.ngs.org.uk

Dasilyron

"Take limitless pains preparing your soil and extreme care positioning your plants. Then let them get on with it."

 # Lutfun's Garden

Gardening is a way of life for community gardener Lutfun Hussain, whose green fingers are busy even when she's off-duty from her work at Spitalfields City Farm (see p.84), and whose home garden frequently wins Tower Hamlets in Bloom awards.

One of her first acts when moving into her home 20 years ago was to plant an apple tree and Lutfun was also able to persuade the council to leave planting spaces for her flowers when they came to pave the front. She speaks for many when she says 'I love a little greenery in the front garden – I didn't want it taken over by the car.'

Lutfun aims for year-round interest, and favours good-looking, easy to care for plants like roses and daffodils to provide seasonal colour and scent. A strong work ethic underpins her gardening, 'When starting a garden work and dig, and people will see the results and get involved. Work is the key.' Lutfun's hands-on approach is contagious: through her gardening she has made friends with her neighbours and has inspired them to grow flowers in their gardens too.

> **When starting a garden work and dig, and people will see the results and get involved. Work is the key."**

Molly's Urban Oasis

The courtyard behind Molly St Hilaire's terraced house in Hackney is petite but perfectly formed. Taking the lush forest clearings of her native Grenada as her inspiration, Molly has created a cosy, contemplative oasis using masses of foliage plants, including ferns and ivy, with robust climbers such as passion flower, roses, wisteria and honeysuckle to build height and add colour. The bold variegation of croton plants (*Codiaeum variegatum*) and the shimmering bamboo are reminders of 'back home' – in Grenada.

The garden's lush abundance is down to Molly: there was nothing in the garden when she moved in nearly 30 years ago. Over the years she has improved the soil with manure and piled on the plants, many propagated by herself. When it comes to pest control, Molly operates a strict zero-tolerance approach to slugs, and keeps the slimy marauders at bay with early morning patrols and swift dispatch in a container of salt.

Although gardening for many years, Molly took it up seriously about 5 years ago when she decided she wanted to join the NGS, and has opened her garden for the last three. Her joy in sharing her garden is evident – bunting and chairs welcome visitors on the street, there are plants for sale, teas and a visitors' book for comments. Molly's love of bright colour manifests itself in her small front garden. Where most people just stash their rubbish bins or bikes, Molly has opted for an exuberant display of hot clashing pink and red flowers. When pressed to recommend a good plant for London gardens, she advocates hydrangeas – 'I think they're nice – you can't go wrong with them.'

Bushberry Road, E9
www.ngs.org.uk

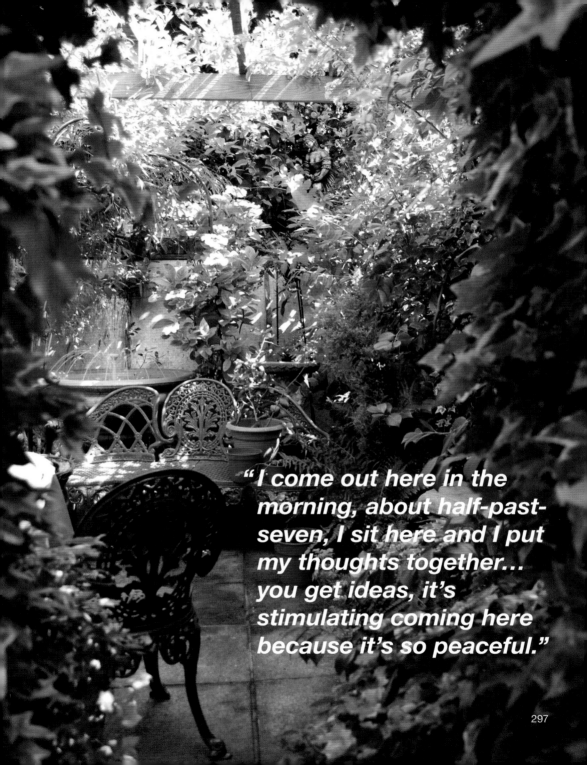

"I come out here in the morning, about half-past-seven, I sit here and I put my thoughts together... you get ideas, it's stimulating coming here because it's so peaceful."

297

"Bird boxes and feeders attract birds to the garden. A nesting blue tit pair eats a lot of garden pests."

The Exotic Garden

Don Map is a man whose passion for plants permeates every inch of his garden. The gardens eclectic mix of tropical plants is partly inspired by his childhood in Belize, partly by a desire to push the boundaries of what he can grow in London.

As for any collector, space is an issue, with Don struggling to squeeze new specimens into his 40 x 16ft garden. Climbing and trailing plants such as the cup and saucer vine (*Cobaea scandens)* and the Brazilian bellflower (*Abutilon megapotamicum*) are one solution. Another tactic is to 'double plant' using the same place to grow one plant in the winter and another in the summer. In this way cuckoopint (*Arum italicum)* might be followed by hostas, or spring flowering American cowslip (*Dodecatheon clevelandii*) yield to summer marigolds. Growing plants in pots means Don can juxtapose ericaceous plants with lime loving ones, achieving combinations that would be impossible in nature, as well as giving him the flexibility to re-arrange his displays.

With juicy tropical plants such as *Brugmansia suaveolens* to tempt them, red spider mite is the garden's main pest, but is controlled with an organic soap-based insecticide. Don warns against making a garden too sterile as he feels this increases pests; he sees weeds as useful allies that can prevent nutrients being washed out from the soil while some, such as the shade-loving Enchanter's nightshade (*Circaea alpina*), make good ground cover plants. Don has got compost making down to a fine art: by using a shredder to speed up the rotting process he harvests his compost every 3 months to enrich his sandy free-draining soil.

For recent NGS openings Don re-planted his front garden on a food, fruit and herbs theme, to show how much can be grown in a small space. Being Don, this showcase included a fruiting lemon tree as well as the unusual double red flowered nasturtium 'Hermine Grashoff'. But when asked to recommend a good London plant Don opts not for exotics but for spring bulbs such as daffodils and native English bluebells.

Maynard Road, E17
www.ngs.org.uk
www.donsgarden.co.uk

The Shady Garden

Like many gardeners, Sybil Caines was bitten by the gardening bug when she acquired her first home. It was a basement flat in Kilburn and she was encouraged by its previous owner to develop the garden. A few years later, and by now an award-winning garden designer (Plantability Garden Design), Sybil was undaunted when it came to taking on the garden at her current home in Stoke Newington.

The garden was a derelict mass of brambles so Sybil developed it from scratch, incorporating the existing trees and some of the old iron fencing that used to extend behind the garden.

Sybil's garden is spacious enough to have distinct areas that perform at different times of the year – the area nearest the house is planted with spring bulbs and hellebores which bloom before the trees come into full leaf and which Sybil can enjoy without having to venture too far into the garden. The garden is also long enough to accommodate a very funky (and award-winning) summerhouse, whose sleek exterior steel wall was designed to reflect the planting and make the garden feel even bigger.

Having a shady garden doesn't dishearten Sybil – there are so many lovely shade-loving plants. She recommends variegated ground cover such as lamiums and pale silver grey *Brunnera macrophylla 'Jack Frost'* to brighten up a dark corner. When picking out good plants for London gardens, Sybil is similarly spoilt for choice. For structural impact she suggests glossy-leaved *Fatsia japonica* or *Mahonia japonica* and she's a big fan of the *Geranium* 'Dusky Crûg', a long flowering perennial with pretty pink flowers and small dark purple leaves that works well as an edging plant.

> **" I get a lot of joy seeing things coming up and opening and I like to do a little tour of my garden every day. Gardening is good for the soul and you get a feel of the seasons as well."**

Despite sharing her garden with all the 'usual suspects' (slugs, snails, lily beetles, squirrels and foxes), Sybil's gardening philosophy is to work with nature. To her this means gardening organically, without slug pellets, and not too tidily – 'it's better for the wildlife'. She also advises being prepared to substitute plants, believing that you can always find another plant that will do the job of the one that never seems to survive or always gets eaten by slugs. She has recently discovered Glebe Nursery in Enfield – 'a lovely nursery where they grow their own plants, and which is really good for perennials.'

Plantability Garden Design
www.chooseplantability.co.uk

Glebe Nursery
Forty Hill, Enfield, Middlesex, EN2 9EU
www.glebenursery.co.uk

Opposite page: Polished steel has been used on the sides of the summerhouse to create the impression of a larger space and reflect more light into the garden.

Cistus x Purpureus 'Alan Fradd'

...unlike a garden which is experienced from 'within', the roundabout is seen by most people only from the outside.

The Magic Roundabout

Caroline Bousfield Gregory has been gardening the Lauriston Road roundabout for over 10 years, transforming it from weedy wasteland to a magical Mediterranean island (albeit one set in a sea of tarmac). She started as a guerrilla gardener but went legit after negotiating a contract – and the usual health and safety hurdles – with the council. It was a shrewd move that has enabled her to tend her prize-winning roundabout with their blessing.

With its drifts of euphorbia, cheery pot marigolds and fragrant lavenders, the garden is a masterclass in the art of low maintenance, low budget gardening. A busy potter (whose workshop is a former stable overlooking the roundabout), Caroline's gardening input varies from half a day each month, to perhaps twice a fortnight. With this in mind, she chooses undemanding, drought tolerant plants that give year-round interest, such as pretty-but-tough cistus and grey-leaved aromatic evergreens like santolina, sage and rosemary. Grasses including the giant reed *Arundo donax* 'Versicolor', as well as phormiums and knifophia, all thrive on the roundabout's savannah like conditions, and add architectural interest. Ease of propagation or a willingness to self seed are also virtues – with excess 'volunteers' being sold to raise funds.

Despite its sunny looks, not everything in the roundabout garden is rosy. Theft and rubbish from passing cars are intermittent problems while the arrival of the rosemary beetle, *Chrysolina americana*, has been a challenge. A voracious green and purple striped pest that devours the leaves of rosemary, lavender and sage, it is the only thing that Caroline sprays against.

Gardening is in Caroline's blood and the wild 'gardens' on the dunes in Cornwall, where her parents lived, have influenced the relaxed feel of the roundabout, where pink and white valerian – a staple of the West Country coastline – flower throughout the summer. The naturalistic look of the roundabout is deceptive, belying the care that Caroline has taken over safety considerations such as the height, density and overhang of plants. Caroline's current planting scheme (instigated in 2004, following disruptive work by the gas board) also acknowledges that, unlike a garden which is experienced from 'within', the roundabout is seen by most people only from the outside. To open up its sightlines, Caroline has installed two gravel paths that bisect the roundabout. These are placed at a diagonal from the road crossings, allow pedestrians to 'see through' the planting to the shops on the other side.

Caroline's public-spirited labours have not gone unnoticed. The roundabout has won prizes in the Hackney in Bloom competition and is supported by the local traders' association. Lavender bags made from flowers harvested on the roundabout and dried using the heat from Caroline's kilns are sold at the local deli. Caroline likes the idea of selling the garden's produce, 'When people buy the lavender bags, its not just a simple purchase, it's a way of supporting the roundabout and, by supporting it, they feel part of it too.'

Caroline Bousfield Gregory
Craftsman Potter, 77a Lauriston Road, E9 7HA
www.carolinebousfield.co.uk

The Pie and Mash Garden

Good fences may make good neighbours but boundaries are an equally important consideration in the small garden. Nina Pope's courtyard garden is blessed with a set of characterful old walls. They are a feature which Nina – an artist and co-designer of What will the Harvest Be? (see p.232) – seeks to accentuate with upwardly mobile wall-trained fruit trees, climbing roses, and passionflower all shown off against the mellow brick.

The garden is unusual, having been created in what was once the fridge-filled backyard of a pie and mash shop in Hackney. With time and space at a premium for Nina, Andrew Dumbleton re-designed the courtyard with low maintenance in mind and with outdoor seating and dining a priority.

Even within a small area growing conditions vary, so containerised plants are moved around the courtyard until they find their 'place'. An advocate of growing from seed, Nina has even successfully raised the notoriously tricky *Meconopsis* (Himalayan blue poppy) and notes that if you grow from seed and the plant dies you get a sense of what's gone wrong, which is not so easy with bought plants. The courtyard's sheltered climate makes it an ideal nursery, although plants tend to get leggy as they reach for the sky. Nina's penchant for dark and silver leaved foliage is not always compatible with a garden that is shaded for most of the day but ferns ('they always look so fresh'), box topiary, black elder, brunnera and heuchera all fit the bill nicely and are thriving.

www.somewhere.org.uk
www.andrewsgardendesign.com
www.chilternseeds.co.uk

"No space is too small – you can do something really nice even with a tiny space."

The Plantsman

This is unashamedly a plantsman's garden. There is no lawn to take up valuable planting space, and precious little in the way of hard landscaping: everything here is geared to the joy of what its owner and creator Charles Rutherfoord describes as 'a growing garden'. For him, 'the whole essence of making a garden, particularly in a city, is greenness. I love Derek Jarman's phrase 'A glimpse of paradise' and I think you only achieve that with plants.'

Charles' own densely planted slice of paradise bursts into spectacular bloom in the spring (when it opens for the NGS). Here visitors can see some 1500 tulips flowering amid irises and tree peonies, while clematis and a pretty pale yellow *Rosa banksiae* 'Lutea' scramble up walls and other supports, and aptly named lilac 'Sensation' struts its stuff.

Confronted by such riches, it's hard to believe when Charles acquired the garden 27 years ago it was 4 feet deep in brambles. A well-

Echium pininana

respected architectural and garden designer, Charles has found that his approach to his garden has evolved over the years, moving from architecturally inspired blocks of acanthus, cistus and ceanothus to experimental plantings of specimens he thought would be exciting to grow. As a result the garden contains a huge number of species, including the biennial Canary Island native *Echium pininana*, the nectar rich honey bush *Melianthus major*, and over 15 species of trees, such as *Acacia parva* (square leafed mimosa) and Wollemi pine. The 'geodetic dome' greenhouse, is the domain of Charles's partner Rupert Tyler, and is filled with succulents and subtropical plants.

The garden has always enjoyed a fertile soil but has a deep annual manure mulch every winter to keep it that way. The mulch goes across everything, and has the pleasing by-product of being very good at suppressing weeds. One plant however has done rather too well for Charles' taste, *Brunnera macrophylla*, which he pulls out by hand where necessary – 'it's very pretty, particularly in the spring, but it is invasive!'

Apart from the pleasure of seeing other people enjoy his garden, Charles likes opening it for the NGS because it makes him look at the garden afresh. Visitors returning year-on-year have spurred him into making changes so there will always be something new for them – 'I think it's really important that the garden should develop.' To this end, Charles has added a late summer open day for the NGS, to showcase his dazzling display of dahlias.

The Chase, Clapham, SW4
www.ngs.org.uk
www.charlesrutherfoord.net

"*Coronilla glauca is one of the best London plants – it flowers right through from late winter until May; it's beautifully scented, and when it's not flowering it's got very beautiful glaucous foliage.*"

311

The Water Garden

Andy Roberts is the gardener at Providence Square, with the unusual responsibility for 'moat management'. This is because the landscaped gardens at the heart of this private residential development near Tower Bridge are encircled by water.

Andy's organic approach extends through the whole garden including using plants as natural filters for the pond water instead of chemicals. A reed bed and generous swathes of marginal plants such as *Caltha palustris* (yellow marsh marigold), *Equisetum scirpoides* (dwarf horsetail), *Houttuynia cordata variegata* (chameleon plant), *Pontaderia cordata* (purple pickerelweed), *Iris pseudacorus* (yellow flag iris) and *Butomis umbellatus* (pink flowering rush); are so effective he no longer uses the installed filtration system. Except for having to break the ice in the winter – the pond now 'takes care of itself'.

Butomis umbellatus (pink flowering rush)

The moat's koi carp thrive on Andy's chemical-free regime, and have voluntarily been joined by ducks, newts, pond skaters, damselflies and backswimmers. Resident foxes and the odd visiting heron are part of the equation too, but Andy takes the resultant duckling and fish losses in his stride – 'that's nature'. Andy's success at encouraging wildlife into the garden has been endorsed with awards from Southwark in Bloom and Bermondsey in Bloom.

A New Zealander, Andy trained as a gardener in London and, after working in the Corporation of London's City gardens, took up his post at Providence Square 3 years ago. Since then he has enhanced the garden's terrestrial planting as well, adding New Zealand natives such as hebe and phormium, and feeding the soil with an annual horse manure mulch. Plants are sourced from Shannon's Garden Centre in Forest Hill, which Andy recommends for its knowledgeable and friendly service.

Andy enjoys developing the gardens in collaboration with the residents, who often pop down for a chat while he is working. Passionate gardener and long-standing Providence Square resident Steve Argles is particularly involved and his planting suggestions, such as crocuses beneath the newly laid lawn and bright blue, self-seeding campanula in the rockery areas, have contributed to the garden's success.

Shannon's Garden Centre
99-105 Stanstead Road, London SE23 1HH
www.shannonsgardencentre.co.uk

"Gardening is a nice job – you don't do it for the money, you do it because you like being outdoors."

Sue's Roof Garden

Chicago may be known as the windy city but London can have its moments too, particularly for those who garden above street level. Sue King Brewster has tended her first floor roof terrace on the Frampton Park Estate for 16 years and has learned a thing or two about what works in breezy conditions.

Windbreaks and weighted containers are advisable while the old 'right plant in the right place' adage holds just as true up here as it does on the ground. Sue has found that alpines, crocosmia, grasses, and waxy leaved plants such as agapanthus are all able to cope with the terrace's microclimate while clematis and passionflower have proved less obliging. The architectural 'foundation' plants that she bought when she first moved in – a cordyline, a palm and a contorted willow – are still thriving, but the garden has evolved a more relaxed style over time, complete with vegetables and a woodlouse friendly log pile.

Growing from seed is a passion for Sue and cottage-garden stalwarts such as cosmos 'Sensation', nasturtiums and night-scented *Nicotiana x sanderae* 'Fragrant Cloud' reciprocate by growing in abundance for her. Unwilling to throw away the excess, Sue sells her seedlings and plants at local fairs and does swaps with friends and neighbours. When it comes to buying for herself she enjoys the World Garden nursery at Lullingstone Castle. It is here she found her favourite plant, the velvet brown – and eminently wind-proof – *Aeonium* 'Chocolate Rose'.

The World Garden Nursery
Lullingstone Castle, Eynsford, Kent, DA4 0JA
www.lullingstonecastle.co.uk

> **If you live in the city everything's so grey, it's really lovely to have your own bit of outside."**

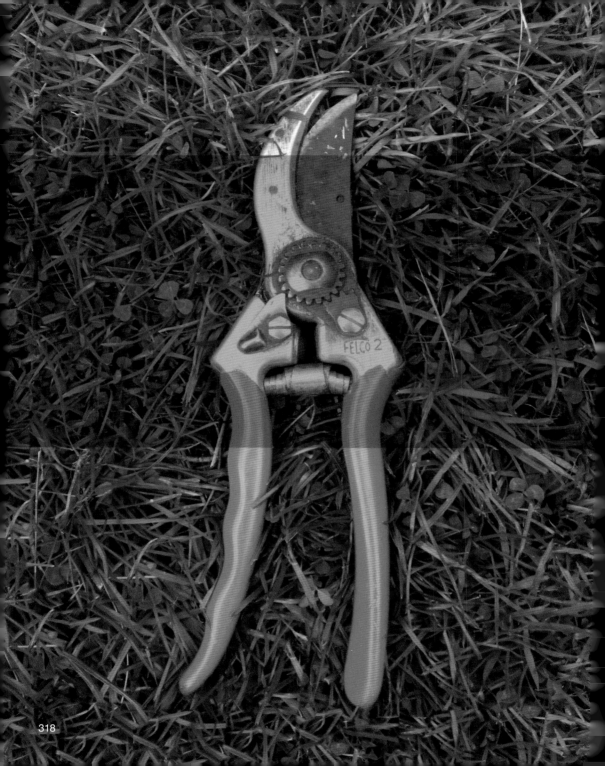

GARDENER'S DIRECTORY

London Horticultural Societies

**Allotment & Kitchen Gardens
(London Borough of Barnet)**
Belmont Lane Allotments & Leisure Gardens
www.belmontlane-allotments.co.uk

Bensham Manor Allotments
www.benshammanorallotments.org.uk

Camberwell Gardens Guild
www.camberwellgardens.guild.org.uk

Chiswick Horticultural Society
www.chsw4.org

De Beauvoir Gardeners Hackney & Islington
www.debeauvoirgardeners.org.uk

Dulwich Society (garden group)
www.dulwichsociety.com/garden-group

Ewell Horticultural Association
www.ewellhortassn.co.uk

Flowers & Plants Association
www.flowers.org.uk

Fulham Horticultural Society
www.fulham-allotments.org

Green Peas
*South London Garden Organic &
Permaculture Group*
www.greenpeasuk.blogspot.com

**Hampstead Garden Suburb
Horticultural society**
www.hgs.org.uk/hortsoc/

Hampstead Horticultural Society
www.hampsteadhorticulturalsociety.org.uk/

The Hardy Plant Society Middlesex Group
www.hardy-plant-middlesex.org.uk

Harrow Horticultural & Rose Society
www.harrowinleaf.org.uk

Headstone Horticultural Society
www.harrowinleaf.org.uk

Islington Gardeners
www.islingtongardeners.org.uk/

Kew Horticultural Society
www.kewhorticulturalsociety.org

Lambeth Horticultural Association
www.lambethhorticulturalsociety.org.uk

London Permaculture
www.londonpermaculturalists.ning.com

Newton Park Horticultural Society
www.harrowinleaf.org.uk

Roehampton Garden Society
www.roehamptonallotments.co.uk

Roxbourne Horticultural society
www.harrowinleaf.org.uk

Spa Hill Organic Gardening Group
www.spahill.org.uk

Streamside Horticultural Association
www.streamside.org.uk

Upminster & District Horticultural Society
www.upminsterhorticulturalsociety.co.uk

Waltham Forest Fuchsia & Pelargonium Society
www.communigate.co.uk/london/fuchsia/

**Whittingham Gardening Club
(Waltham Forest)**
www.communigate.co.uk/london/
whittinghamgardeningclub

Allotments

Alric Avenue Allotments Association
www.alricallotments.com

**Barnet Federation of Allotment
& Horticultural Societies**
www.bfahs.org

Belmont Lane Allotments & Leisure Gardens
www.belmontlane-allotments.co.uk

Bensham Manor Allotments
www.benshammanorallotments.org.uk

**Bexley Federation of Allotment
& Leisure Gardeners**
www.bfalg.co.uk

Bexley Council Allotments
www.bexley.gov.uk

Clifford Road Allotments (Barnet)
www.crallotments.org.uk

Croydon Council Allotments
www.croydon.gov.uk
Croydon Federation of Allotment &
Leisure Garden Societies

Ealing Allotments Partnership
www.ealingallotmentspartnership.co.uk

Eltham Allotments & Garden Society
www.eags.org.uk

**Fulham Palace Meadows Allotments
Association**
www.fulham-allotments.org

Great London Allotments Forum
www.londonallotments.net

Hackney Allotments
www.hackneyallotments.org.uk

Harland Avenue Sidcup Allotment Society
www.hasas.org.uk

Harrow in Leaf (Umbrella organization for Allotments in Hackney)
www.harrowinleaf.org.uk

Hillingdon Allotment & Horticultural Federation
www.hahf.org.uk

Kent House Leisure Gardens Association
www.khlga.com

Manor Gardens
www.lifeisland.org

North Finchley Allotments (Barnet)
www.northfinchleyallotments.org

One Tree Hill Allotments (Southwark)
www.othas.org.uk

Park Hill Allotments (Croydon)
www.parkhill-allotments.org.uk

Roehampton Garden Society
www.roehamptonallotments.co.uk

Romford Smallholders Society
www.romfordsmallholderssociety.org.uk

Rosendale Road Allotments (Lambeth)
www.tam.southspace.org.uk/wordpress

Royal Paddocks Allotments (Hampton Court)
www.www.paddocks-allotments.org.uk

Spa Hill Allotment Society Ltd
www.spahill.org.uk

Vale Farm Allotment Society (Barnet)
www.valefarmproject.co.uk

West Ham Allotments
www.westhamallotments.org.uk

Windmill Allotments (Brixton Hill)
www.windmillallotments.org.uk

Woodhouse Allotments (Barnet)
www.woodhouseontheweb.org.uk

London Allotments Network
www.londonallotments.net

South Croydon Allotment Society Ltd
www.south-croydon-allotments.org.uk

West Harrow Allotment & Garden Association
www.harrowinleaf.org.uk/whaga.html

Woodside Addiscombe & Shirley Allotment Society
www.awslg.org.uk

Garden Blogs & Web Resources

www.outofmyshed.co.uk

www.fennelandfern.co.uk

www.helenbabbs.wordpress.com

www.blog.lauranolte.com

www.guerrillagardening.org

www.somewhere.org.uk/blog

www.waywardplants.org

www.verticalveg.org.uk

Organisations

Allotments Regeneration Initiative
www.farmgarden.org.uk

Alpine Garden Society
www.alpinegardensociety.net

Association of Garden Trusts
www.gardenstrusts.org.uk

British Beekeepers' Association
www.britishbee.org.uk
For more beekeeping resources, see p.25

Capital Growth
www.capitalgrowth.org

The Cottage Garden Society
www.thecottagegardensociety.org.uk

E A Bowles of Myddelton House Society
www.eabowlessociety.org.uk

Federation of City Farms & Community Gardens
www.farmgarden.org.uk

Green Chain Walk
www.greenchain.com

The Hardy Plant Society
www.hardy-plant.org.uk

The Herb Society
www.herbsociety.org.uk

Garden History Society
www.gardenhistorysociety.org

Garden Organic
www.gardenorganic.org.uk

Gardening Leave – gardening therapy for forces veterans
www.gardeningleave.org

Greenfingers
www.greenfingerscharity.org.uk

Japanese Garden Society
www.jgs.org.uk

Landshare
www.landshare.net

Linnaean Society of London
www.linnean.org

London Children's Flower Society
www.lcfs.olaves.net

London in Bloom
www.londoninbloom.co.uk

London Wildlife Trust
www.wildlondon.org.uk/
For more wildlife resources, see p.241

Mediterranean Garden Society (UK branch)
www.mediterraneangardensociety.org

National Council for the Conservation of Plants & Gardens
www.nccpg.com

National Gardens Scheme
www.ngs.org.uk

National Society of Allotment & Leisure Gardeners Ltd
www.nsalg.org.uk

National Trust
www.nationaltrust.org.uk

National Vegetable Society
www.nvsuk.org.uk

Naturewise London
(permaculture, forest gardens)
www.naturewise.org.uk

(NCCPG) Plant Heritage
www.nccpg.com

The Old Lawnmower Club
www.oldlawnmowerclub.co.uk

Perennial: Gardeners' Royal Benevolent Society
www.perennial.org.uk

Professional Gardeners' Guild
www.pgg.org.uk

Project Dirt
www.projectdirt.com

Royal Horticultural Society
www.rhs.org.uk

Seedy Sunday
(seed exchange event in Brighton & Hove)
www.seedysunday.org

Society of Garden Designers
www.sgd.org.uk

Soil Association
www.soilassociation.org

Sydenham Garden
www.sydenhamgarden.org.uk

Thrive
www.thrive.org.uk

Trees for Cities
www.treesforcities.org

Woodland Trust
www.woodlandtrust.org.uk

Open Garden Squares Weekend celebrates London's secret outdoor spaces, giving you priviledged access to gardens and squares not normally open to the public. It takes place every year during the 2nd weekend of June.. One weekend ticket provides access to numerous gardens and squares in London not usually open to the public. Parks and gardens put on special events, such as jazz bands, all contributing to that festive atmosphere. See our website for more information:

www.opensquares.org

OPEN GARDEN SQUARES WEEKEND

in association with the **National Trust**

London Parks & Gardens Trust

Garden Events

JANUARY:

London's Charity Potato Fair & Seed Exchange
www.potatofair.og

FEBRUARY:

RHS Orchid Show & RHS Botanical Art Show

MARCH:

RHS London Greener Gardening Show

APRIL:

Spring Gardening Show, Capel Manor

MAY:

RHS Chelsea Flower Show *(p.50)*
Chelsea Fringe *(p.54)*

**International Sunflower Guerrilla
Gardening Day** *(p.110)*

JUNE:

London Open Garden Squares Weekend *(p.170)*
www.opensquares.org
www.londongardenstrust.org

JULY:

RHS Hampton Court Flower Show *(p.118)*

AUGUST:

Kew Summer Show

SEPTEMBER:

The Spitalfields Show & Green Fair
Spitalfields City Farm

City Harvest Festival, Capel Manor *(p.34)*

OCTOBER:

RHS London Autumn Harvest Show

Calthorpe Project, London Open Garden Squares Weekend, see p.170

Garden Centres

North

Alexandra Palace Garden Centre
Alexandra Palace Way, N22 4BB
www.capitalgardens.co.uk
Tel: 020 8444 2555

Boma Garden Centre
52-53 Islip Street, NW5 2DL
www.bomagardencentre.co.uk
Tel: 020 7284 4999

Camden Garden Centre
2 Barker Drive, St Pancras Way, NW1 0JW
www.camdengardencentre.co.uk
Tel: 020 7387 7080

Highgate Garden Centre
Highgate High St, 1 Townsend Yard, N6 5JF
www.capitalgardens.co.uk
Tel: 020 8340 1041

John's Garden Centre
175 Stoke Newington Church St, N16 0UL
www.johns-gardencentre.co.uk
Tel: 020 7275 9494

Moyses Stevens
788a Finchley Road, NW11 7TJ
www.moysesflowers.co.uk
Tel: 020 8772 0094

North One Garden Centre
The Old Button Factory, 25 Englefield Rd, N1 4EU
www.n1gc.co.uk
Tel: 020 7923 3553

Sunshine Garden Centre
Durnsford Road, Bounds Green, N11 2EL
www.sunshinegardencentre.co.uk
Tel: 020 8889 4224

West

The Chelsea Gardener
125 Sydney Street, SW3 6NR
www.chelseagardener.com
Tel: 020 7352 5656

Clifton Nurseries
5A Clifton Villas, W9 2PH
www.clifton.co.uk
Tel: 020 7289 6851

Fulham Palace Garden Centre
Bishop's Avenue, SW6 6EE
www.fulhamgardencentre.com
Tel: 020 7736 2640

C Rassells
78-80 Earls Court Road, W8 6EQ
Tel: 020 7937 0481

W6 Garden Centre
Ravenscourt Avenue, W6 0SL
Tel: 020 8563 7112
www.w6gc.co.uk

World's End Nurseries
441-457 King's Road, SW10 0LR
www.worldsendnurseries.com
Tel: 020 7351 3343

South-West

Neals Nurseries Garden Centre
Heathfield Road, SW18 2PH
www.capitalgardens.co.uk
Tel: 020 8874 2037

Sheen Garden Centre
Adrian Hall Garden Centres,
181-189 Upper Richmond Road West,
East Sheen, SW14 8DU
www.adrianhall.co.uk/sheen-garden-centre
Tel: 020 8876 3648

Tubby' outdoor sofa and armchair... Part of 2012 contemporary garden range.

www.bau-outdoors.co.uk
0800 046 3456

South-East

Alexandra Nurseries
Estate House, Parish Lane, Penge, SE20 7LJ
www.alexandranurseries.co.uk
Tel: 0208 778 4145

Alleyn Park Garden Centre
77 Park Hall Road, SE21 8ES
www.alleynpark.co.uk
Tel: 020 8670 7788

Bexley Garden Centre
1-3 Basildon Road, Abbey Wood, SE2 0ET
www.bexleygardencentre.org.uk
Tel: 020 8311 5212

Hortus
26 Blackheath Village, SE3 9SY
www.hortus-london.com
Tel: 020 8297 9439

Phoebe's Garden Centre
2 Penerley Road, SE6 2LQ
www.phoebes.co.uk
Tel: 020 8698 4365

Secret Garden Centre
70 Westow St, Crystal Palace, SE19 3AF
www.thesecretgardencentre.com
Tel: 020 8771 8200

Shannons Garden Centre
99-105 Standstead Road, SE23 1HH
www.shannonsgardencentre.co.uk
Tel: 020 8291 1502

East

Growing Concerns
2 Wick Lane, E2 2NA
www.growingconcerns.org
Tel: 020 8985 322

Outskirts

Bexley Garden Centre
57 North Cray Road, Sidcup, DA14 5EU
www.bexleygardencentre.org.uk
Tel: 020 8309 1442

Wood's of Berkhamsted Garden Centre,
High Street, Berkhamsted, Herts, HP4 1BJ
www.capitalgardens.co.uk
01442 863 159

Morden Hall Garden Centre
Morden Hall Road, Morden, Surrey, SM4 5JD
www.capitalgardens.co.uk
Tel: 020 8646 3002

Petersham Nurseries
Church Lane, 143 Petersham Road,
Richmond, TW10 7AG
www.petershamnurseries.com
Tel: 020 8940 5230

Squires of the Kiln
Common Road, Stanmore, Middlesex, HA7 3JF
www.squiresgardencentres.co.uk
Tel: 020 8954 4628

Squires Garden Centre
Sixth Cross Rd, Twickenham, Middlesex, TW2 5PA
www.squiresgardencentres.co.uk
Tel: 020 8977 9241

Squires Garden Centre
Halliford Road, Shepperton, Middlesex, TW17 8SG
www.squiresgardencentres.co.uk
Tel: 01932 784 121

Thompsons Plant and Garden Centre
Nutty Lane, Shepperton, Middlesex, TW17 0RQ
www.thompsons-plants.co.uk
Tel: 01932 781 474

Ruxley Manor Garden Centre
Maidstone Road, Sidcup, DA14 5BQ
www.ruxley-manor.co.uk
Tel: 020 8300 0084

Community Gardens, City Farms & Nature Reserves

Bankside Open Spaces Trust
Junction of King James St & Library St, SE1
www.bost.org.uk
Tel: 020 7261 1009

Brockwell Park Community Greenhouses
Brockwell Park, SE24
www.brockwellparkcommunitygreenhouses.
org.uk
Tel: 020 7622 4913

Bromley by Bow Gardens
Corner of St Leonard's St & Grace St, E3
www.bbbc.org.uk
Tel: 020 8709 9735

Brooks Farm
Skeltons Lane Park, E10
Tel: 020 8539 4278

Cable Street Community Garden
Hardinge Street, E1
www.cablestreetcommunitygardens.co.uk

Calthorpe Project Community Garden
Corner of Gray's Inn Road & Ampton St, WC1
www.calthorpeproject.org.uk
Tel: 020 7837 8019

Camley Street Natural Park
Off Camley St, NW1
Tel: 020 7833 2311
www.wildlondon.org.uk

Capel Manor College
Bullsmoor Lane, Enfield, Middlesex, EN1
www.capelmanorgardens.org.uk
Tel: 08456 122 122

Community & Environment Project Office
(Edmonton)
www.cepo.btik.com
Tel: 01992 701 438

Spitalfields' City Farm

Coram's Fields
Guilford Street, WC1
www.coramsfields.org
Tel: 020 7837 6138

Culpeper Community Garden
Jct Cloudesley Rd & Copenhagen St, N1
www.culpeper.org.uk
Tel: 020 7833 3951

Deen City Farm
Off Windsor Avenue, SW9
www.deencityfarm.co.uk
Tel: 020 8543 5300

Devonshire Road Nature Reserve
170 Devonshire Rd, Forest Hill, SE23
www.devonshireroadnaturereserve.org

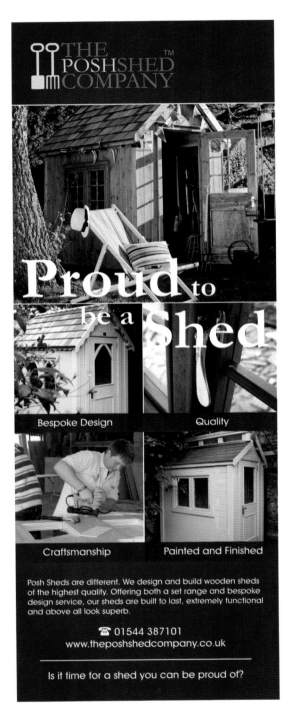

Eden at St Pauls Community Garden
Rectory Grove, SW4
www.stpaulssw4.org/eden-garden
Tel: 020 7498 3810

The Edible Bus Stop
www.theediblebusstop.org

Forest Farm Peace Garden
Hazelbrouck Gardens, Hainault, IG6
www.forestfarmpeacegarden.org
Tel: 020 8252 0201

Freightliners Farm
Sheringham Road (next to Paradise Park), N7
www.freightlinersfarm.org.uk
Tel: 020 7609 0467

Growing Communities
Sites in N16 & E5
www.growingcommunities.org
Tel: 020 7502 7588

Grow Mayow Community Garden
Mayow Park, Mayow Rd, Sydenham, SE26
www.growmayow.blogspot.com
Tel: 020 8291 6596

Hackney City Farm
Goldsmith's Row, off Hackney Rd, E2
www.hackneycityfarm.co.uk
Tel: 020 7729 6381

Hackney Community Tree Nursery & Edible Forest Garden
Hackney Marsh
www.hackneyenvironment.org.uk/TNFG

Hammersmith Community Gardens Association
(Loris Road Community Garden, Godolphin Garden & Ravenscourt Park Greenhouses), W12
www.hcga.org.uk
Tel: 07890 514 050

Harleyford Road Community Garden
Harleyford Road, SW8
Tel: 020 7485 5001

Heart Garden
Chumleigh Gardens, Burgess Park, Albany Rd, SE5
www.artinthepark.co.uk
Tel: 020 7277 4297

Heathrow Special Needs Farm
Bath Road, Longford, UB7 0EF
www.heathrowspecialneedsfarm.co.uk
Tel: 01753 680 330

Hounslow Urban Farm
Faggs Road, Feltham, TW14
www.hounslow.info/parks/urbanfarm
Tel: 020 8831 9658

Hoxton Trust Community Garden
Hoxton Street, N1
www.hoxtontrust.com/community/htm
Tel: 020 7729 1480

Kentish Town City Farm
Cressfield Close, off Grafton Road, NW5
www.ktcityfarm.org.uk
Tel: 020 7916 5421

King Henry's Walk Garden
11c King Henry's Walk, N1
www.khwgarden.org.uk
Tel: 020 7923 9035

Lambourne End Outdoor Centre
Manor Road, Lambourne End, Essex, RM4 1NB
www.lambourne-end.org.uk
Tel: 020 8500 3047

Maiden Lane Community Enterprises
156 Maiden Lane, NW1
www.maidenlanece.org
Tel: 020 7267 9586

Meanwhile Gardens & Mind Wildlife Garden
154 & 156-158 Kensal Road, W10
www.meanwhilegardens.com
Tel: 020 8960 4600 (Meanwhile)
Tel: 020 8960 6336 (Mind)

Mudchute Park & Farm
Pier Street, E14
www.mudchute.org
Tel: 020 7515 5901

Newham City Farm
Stansfeld Road, E6
www.newhamcityfarm.org
Tel: 020 7474 4960

Oasis Children's Nature Garden
Corner Larkhall Lane & Studley Road, SW4
www.oasisplay.org.uk
Tel: 020 7498 2329

Phoenix Garden
Corner St Giles Passage & New Compton St, WC2
www.phoenixgarden.org
Tel: 020 7379 3187

Poets Corner Garden
Corner Chaucer Road & Myrtle Road, W3
Tel: 020 7485 5001

Roe Green Walled Garden
Roe Green Park, NW9
www.bhcg.ik.com
Tel: 020 8206 0492

Roots & Shoots Wildlife Garden
Walnut Tree Walk, SE11
www.rootsandshoots.org.uk
Tel: 020 7587 1131

St Mary's Secret Garden
Corner Pearson Street & Appleby Street, E2
www.stmaryssecretgarden.org.uk
Tel: 020 7739 2965

Spitalfields City Farm
Pedley Street, E1
www.spitalfieldscityfarm.org
Tel: 020 7247 8762

Sunnyside Community Gardens
Jct Sunnyside Road & Hazelville Road, N19
www.sunnysidegarden.org.uk
Tel: 020 7272 3522

Surrey Docks Farm
Rotherhithe Street, SE16
www.surreydocksfarm.org.uk
Tel: 020 7231 1010

Sutton Ecology Centre
The Old Rectory, Festival Walk, Carshalton, SM5
www.sutton.gov.uk
Tel: 020 8770 5820

Sydenham Gardens
Holland Drive, off Queenswood Road, SE23
www.sydenhamgarden.org.uk
Tel: 020 8291 1650

The Gardens Community Garden
Doncaster & Stanhope Gardens,
off Green Lanes, N4
www.gardensresidents.blogspot.com
Tel: 020 8374 7721

Vauxhall City Farm
Tyers Street, SE11
www.vauxhallcityfarm.org
Tel: 020 7582 4204

Walworth Garden Farm
Corner Manor Place & Braganza Street, SE17
www.walworthgardenfarm.org.uk
Tel: 020 7582 2652

Wellgate Community Farm
Collier Row Road, Romford, RM5 2BH
www.wellgatefarm.org
Tel: 01708 747850

Woodlands Farm Trust
331 Shooters Hill, Kent, DA16 3RP
www.thewoodlandsfarmtrust.org
Tel: 020 8319 8900

Alexandra Nurseries, Penge, see p.327

Community Orchards

The London Orchard Project
www.thelondonorchardproject.org

Hackney Harvest
www.hackneyharvest.com

Common Ground
www.commonground.org.uk

Blondin Community Orchard
www.friendsofblondin.org.uk

Butterfield Green Community Orchard
www.shakespeareresidents.org.uk

Chinbrook Community Orchard
www.lewisham.gov.uk

Green Peppers Orchard & Forest Garden
www.maidenlanece.org

Lambeth Walk Open Space Community Garden
www.rootsandshoots.org.uk

LEAF Community Orchard
Camberwell

Marks Gate Community Orchard
Barking & Dagenham

Melbourne Grove Urban Orchard
Dulwich

The Nubian Life Resources Centre
www.nubian-life.org.uk

Stave Hill Ecology Park
Rotherhithe
www.urbanecology.org.uk

GARDEN MUSEUM

celebrates the design, history & art of gardens

with a permanent gardening exhibition, regular temporary exhibitions, the only specialist garden bookshop in London and a wonderful garden café

www.gardenmuseum.org.uk

Lambeth Palace Rd, SE1 7LB
Tel: 020 7401 8865
Fax: 020 7401 8869
info@gardenmuseum.org.uk

Open daily: 10.30am-5.00pm
(Saturday closes 4.00pm)

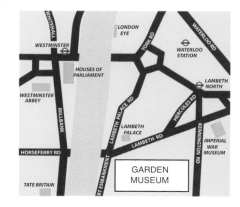

Bibliography

London's Parks & Gardens – Billington, Jill (Frances Lincoln, 2003)

The Allotment Book – Clevely, Andi (Collins, 2006)

Gardens of England, Scotland and Wales, A Guide and Gazetteer – Evans, Hazel (George Philip Ltd, 1991)

Directions for the Gardiner and other Horticultural Advice (edited Maggie Campbell-Culver) – Evelyn, John (Oxford University Press, 2009)

A garden from a hundred packets of seed – Fenton, James (Penguin 2001)

London's Natural History, Fitter, Richard (Collins 1945)

London's Pride The Glorious History of the Capital's Gardens – Galinou, Mireille (ed) (Anaya Publishers Ltd, 1990)

The Story of Gardening – Hobhouse, Penelope (Dorling Kindersley, 2002)

The Cable Street Gardeners – Kelly, Chris (CK Editions, 2005)

The London Town Garden – Longstaffe-Gowan (Yale University Press, 2001)

Flora Britannica The Concise Edition – Mabey, Richard (Chatto & Windus, 1998)

The Gardener's London – Macleod, Dawn (Gerard Duckworth, 1972)

London Gardens A Seasonal Guide – Parker, Lorna (Watling Street Publishing 2004)

Forgotten Fruits – Stocks, Christopher (Random House, 2008)

A Little History of British Gardening – Uglow, Jenny (Chatto & Windus, 2004)

Allotments – Way, Twigs (Shire Publications, 2010)

The Brother Gardeners – Wulf, Andrea (William Heinemann, 2008)

Hampton Court Flower Show, see p.118

Index

Other Metro titles....

LONDON'S HIDDEN WALKS
THE LONDON WE KNOW IS JUST THE SURFACE!

Volume 1

LONDON'S HOUSES
FROM WORKHOUSE TO ROYAL PALACE, COME IN, CLOSE THE DOOR AND STEP BACK IN TIME...

LONDON'S CITY CHURCHES
SEE THE SCORCH MARKS OF THE GREAT FIRE, OR VISIT AN ALTAR BY HENRY MOORE

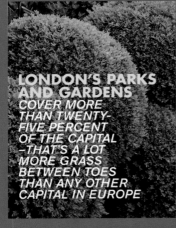

LONDON'S PARKS AND GARDENS
COVER MORE THAN TWENTY-FIVE PERCENT OF THE CAPITAL –THAT'S A LOT MORE GRASS BETWEEN TOES THAN ANY OTHER CAPITAL IN EUROPE

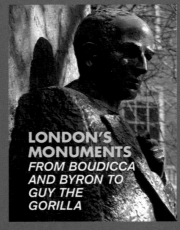

LONDON'S MONUMENTS
FROM BOUDICCA AND BYRON TO GUY THE GORILLA

LONDON'S CEMETERIES
SPEND THE DAY WITH KARL MARX, ENID BLYTON, KEITH MOON AND MANY MORE

FOOD LOVERS' LONDON
Jenny Linford

'A JOY'
Nigel Slater

LONDON ARCHITECTURE
MARIANNE BUTLER (foreword by Maxwell Hutchinson)

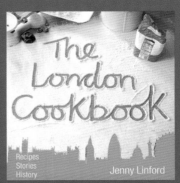

The London Cookbook

Recipes
Stories
History

Jenny Linford

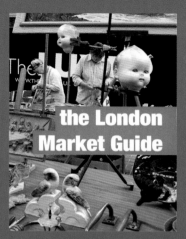

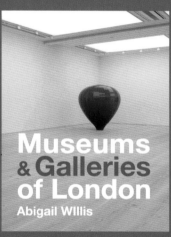

About us:

Metro is an independent publishing company with a reputation for producing well-researched and beautifully-designed guides on many aspects of London life. In fields of interest as diverse as shopping, bargain hunting, architecture, the arts, and food, our guide books contain special tips you won't find anywhere else.

The following titles are available to buy from our website. Alternatively, you can call our customer order line on 020 8533 7777 (Visa/Mastercard/Switch)

www.metropublications.com

Image Credits

Author Portrait © Wendy Edwards; p.2 © Christian Koch; p.4-p.6 © Stephen Millar; p.48 © Wildlife Centre; p.55 © Chelsea Fringe; p.56-p.58 Stephen Millar; p.60-p.63 © Chiswick House; p.94, p.95 © Stephen Millar; p.98, p.99 © Adrian Pope; p.122 © Michelle Duxbury; p.123 © Nigel Clifford; p.124 © Christian Koch; p.126, p.127 © Royal Historic Palaces; p.132 © Laura Mtungwazi; p.133 © Caroline Hughes; p.140, p.141, p.143 © Virgin Limited Edition and The Roof Gardens; p.145 © RBG Kew Garden; p.153 © Laura Nolte; p.164 © Roger Phillips; p.174 © Petersham Nurseries, p.180-p.181 © Josef Coates – Davis; p.194 © Franchi Seeds; p.216, p.217 © London Underground, p.221 © Sarah Cuttle; p.230-p.231© Stephen Millar; p.250-p.254 © RBG Kew Garden; p.261 © The Gentle Author of www.spitalfieldslife. com; p.289 © Acres Wild Ltd; p.305 © Gary Manhine.

Victoria Park in winter